BRAIN BUSTERS!

Mind-Stretching Puzzles in Math and Logic

BARRY R. CLARKE

R	A	N	T
R	I	F	E
D	A	M	E
T	I	M	E

DOVER PUBLICATIONS, INC.
Mineola, New York

Acknowledgments

I would like to thank Val Gilbert, Puzzles Editor at *The Daily Telegraph* (UK), for providing a reason to create these puzzles and John Grafton at Dover Publications, Inc., for the opportunity to create this work.

Bibliographical Note

Brain Busters! Mind-Stretching Puzzles in Math and Logic is a new work, first published by Dover Publications, Inc., in 2003.

Library of Congress Cataloging-in-Publication Data

Clarke, Barry R.
   Brain busters! : mind-stretching puzzles in math and logic / Barry R. Clarke.
      p. cm.
   ISBN 0-486-42755-2 (pbk.)
   1. Mathematical recreations. 2. Logic, Symbolic and mathematical. I. Title.

QA95.C53 2003
793.7'4—dc21

2003046068

Manufactured in the United States of America
Dover Publications, Inc., 31 East 2nd Street, Mineola, N.Y. 11501

CONTENTS

INTRODUCTION

WELCOME to *Brain Busters!* Next time you see your brilliant mathematical friend, give him these to try. Did he know that square is a square? Of course he did, but given that fact, can he say what length each side has to be? Did he also know that it's possible to make one straight cut to a tetrahedron, a pyramid with a triangular base, to make two identical cubes? "Impossible!" he will cry, but watch him turn blue when you announce you know how to do it! The solutions to these and many other challenging puzzles lie within these covers and can be yours for the price of a good meal out—and there's much more to chew over!

Many of the puzzles in this book have been selected from my column in *The Daily Telegraph* (UK), some are taken from my book *Test Your Puzzle Power,* and the rest are published here for the first time. A wide variety of problems of varying difficulty appear, including word, logic, algebraic, matchstick, and lateral; in fact, it's fair to say that there's something for everyone. The book is divided into three sections: Popular Puzzles, Teaser Tales, and Advanced Puzzles. The Popular Puzzles can be solved with a moderate amount of effort and imagination. This section also includes Complex Crosswords where cryptic clues must be solved in sequence and the solutions fitted together on a blank grid, rather like a jigsaw. Great fun—and there's an easy-to-understand Tutorial to help you solve the cryptic clues (as well as some of the logic puzzles). If you're not a regular crossword solver, don't worry: there are only a small number of different clue types, which are fully explained, and reliance on general knowledge is kept to a minimum. The Teaser Tales are longer than the Popular Puzzles and take the form of entertaining stories where all the clues must be solved to get a single solution at the end. Finally, the Advanced Puzzles are designed to stretch those puzzle geniuses who enjoy a real challenge. Despite being more mathematical than the other puzzles, no greater knowledge than high school algebra is required, however, they will take you to the edge!

Each puzzle has a hint and solution, both identified by a number at the bottom of the page (e.g., Hint 6; Solution 29). These appear out of sequence in the Hints and Solutions so that you can avoid accidentally seeing those for the next puzzle. The Teaser Tales, being of only moderate difficulty, have no hints, only solutions.

Have you ever wondered why puzzle compilers compile? Creating problems for people to solve seems to do little for humanity's struggle with nature; after all, there are already plenty of unsolved problems to turn our minds to without adding others (e.g., what exactly *is* electric charge?). Every compiler has his or her own reasons. Some will say they want to entertain; others will claim they want to exercise your mind. But for me, it is neither. I simply want to create art, original and finely crafted art, through the poetry of logic and mathematics—lines that, with sufficient clues, you too can recreate. If you are entertained by these puzzles, that is fine. If you find exercise for your mind, that is fine too. However, if you can experience that craftsman's joy that I felt on constructing some of these puzzles, then this book will have been worthwhile.

Oh, and before you turn blue, the solution to the square and tetrahedron puzzles can be found at the end of the book (Solution 52)!

BARRY R. CLARKE

Oxford, UK
puzzledbarry@yahoo.co.uk
http://barryispuzzled.com

TUTORIAL

THIS easy-to-understand tutorial is designed to help you solve some of the puzzles that follow.

Liar Puzzle

The liar puzzle is a logic problem consisting of several statements with the condition that only a given number of them are true. It is the task of the solver to deduce reliable information from each statement. Here is a typical case.

Exactly one of James, Andrea, or Francis has money. James says, "Andrea does not have money"; Andrea says, "Neither James nor myself has money"; Francis says, "Either James or Andrea has money." If precisely one of them is truthful, who has money?

When we assume that someone is being truthful, we assume that he really experiences what he claims to experience. However, when we assume that someone lies, we assume that his experience is the opposite of what he claims it to be. So let's make a table of the experiences that each person must have had for the two cases of truth teller and liar. In this particular puzzle, the experience is about who has money.

Name	Truth teller	Liar
James	F or J	A
Andrea	F	J or A
Francis	J or A	F

Now, everyone must know who has the money. It's just that those who lie are attempting to conceal what they know. So in this table of possible real experiences, we seek a True/False/False combination where the same person appears in all three. This must be the culprit. The only way this can occur is if Francis is the truth teller and the rest are liars, so that Andrea appears in all three and thus has the money. This problem has many variations, but the principle is always the same.

Logic Tables

The Popular Puzzles section also has another kind of logic problem where a table is given—for example, house number, first name, and surname—and although each item appears in the correct column, only one in each column is correctly matched with the left-hand column. The aim is to match all items correctly.

House	First Name	Surname
1	John	Tibble
2	Susan	Cabbage
3	Gary	Simpson

Some relations between elements are also given which allow the solver to piece together the solution. Let's have the following relations. Susan does not live at number 1 and is neither Cabbage nor Tibble. Tibble does not live at number 2.

A good way to approach this problem is to make a table of possible positions and draw out any additional relations as jigsaw pieces.

House	First Name	Surname
1	John/Gary	
2		Cabbage/Simpson
3		

Additional piece : Susan   Simpson

We can now start to make deductions with the table and piece(s), and in doing so, arrive at all the possible ways the pieces can fit the table. Now, the additional piece cannot be at house number 1 due to the possible first names there, so it must be at 2 or 3.

House	First Name	Surname
1	John/Gary	
2		Cabbage/Simpson
3	Susan	Simpson

Suppose Susan Simpson is at 3. This means that Simpson was correctly positioned at 3 originally, so Cabbage was wrong at 2 and Tibble was wrong at 1 (remember, only one can be correctly positioned originally). So Tibble can only be at 2, which leads to a contradiction with our table. So our assumption that Susan Simpson is at 3 is incorrect.

House	First Name	Surname
1	John/Gary	
2	Susan	Simpson
3		

Suppose Susan Simpson is at 2. Then Susan was correctly positioned at 2 originally (so the other two were wrongly located) and Gary must be at 1 with John at 3. For the surname, if Simpson is at 2, then both Simpson and Cabbage must have been wrongly positioned originally. So Tibble was correct at 1 and Cabbage is at 3.

House	First Name	Surname
1	Gary	Tibble
2	Susan	Simpson
3	John	Cabbage

As these puzzles increase in difficulty (and they do!), those who enjoy a challenge should be well rewarded!

Complex Crosswords

The clues in the Complex Crosswords are easier than ordinary cryptic crosswords. However, some work is needed to work out where the solutions fit in. There are ten cryptic clues for each one, and as you find each word in sequence, it must be placed on the 10x10 grid to overlap a previously found word or words (except for the first solution which can be placed anywhere). The solutions are placed across and down *alternately,* and when positioning them, you may create other valid words coincidentally. However, no nonword is allowed, intentionally or otherwise. When the grid has been correctly completed, it should be possible to fit in the extra word AXE across.

While there may be several ways of fitting in the clue solutions, there is only one way to arrive at a word pattern that the word AXE fits into across. So for each Complex Crossword, the question arises: Where does the AXE fall?! Hints accompany each clue in case things get a bit difficult.

So let's have a look at how the Complex Crossword works. Let us suppose that the first four solutions were CARROT, BAILIFF, SINGER, and PART alternating across and down. There is only one way to combine BAILIFF with CARROT and only one way to fit SINGER with BAILIFF. However, there are two ways that PART can be fitted in as shown.

```
                                                          P
                P                                         A
        B       A                       B                 R
  C     A   R   R   O   T          C    A    R    R    O   T
        I       T                       I
        L                               L
  S     I   N   G   E   R          S    I    N    G    E   R
        F                               F
        F                               F
```

Note that PART can fit onto neither the first R in CARROT nor the R in SINGER without creating a nonword. The variations that occur must all be kept in view as the crossword progresses.

To those people who feel that crosswords are beyond them, fear not! There are only a handful of clue types that occur, and these are as follows.

Letters in sequence

Intense, some actor ridiculed (6)

In most cases, the clue word or words appear first. So in this instance we want a word that means the same as *intense*. The "some" indicator tells us that the solution letters appear in sequence in the words following the indicator.

The number in parentheses shows the number of required letters. So the solution appears in "acTOR RIDiculed" as TORRID.

Letters in reverse sequence

Zest, reflecting on tarot suggestion (5)

The presence of the "reflecting on" indicator points to letters appearing in reverse order in "tarot suggestion." Equivalent indicators are "returning from/with," "back from/with," or anything that implies reversal. The solution here is GUSTO.

Letters in sequence with included/excluded letters

Post, some man stamps, not Nigel initially (4)

Variations on the first two examples involve the inclusion or exclusion of letters from the solution sequence. A negative indicator such as "not," "without," or "lacking" denotes exclusion, while "with" or any additive idea denotes inclusion. The letters involved then follow the indicator. When a single letter is involved, the indicator "initially" or "at first" points to the first letter(s) of the word(s) that follow the inclusion/exclusion indicator. The present example gives MAnST, which would be MAST except for the "n." However, "not Nigel initially" informs us that this letter should be excluded.

Anagram with included letters

Period, in torment (4)

The absence of an indicator or the indicator "in" should alert you to an anagram. In this case, the letters "torment" include the four letters of a word meaning *period,* that is, TERM.

Anagram with excluded letters

Suspend, no ice ceilings (5)

Here the "no" indicator alerts one to the removal of letters. The letters ICE taken from CEILING gives SLING on rearrangement, another word for *suspend.*

Initial letters of words

"No original idea seems exciting at first," uttered loudly.

The "at first" indicator shows that first letters must be selected, and we have a rare case where the clue words "uttered loudly" are not at the beginning. The first letters of the first five words spell NOISE.

It is a characteristic of the Complex Crosswords that appear here that all the letters that are required for the solution word are contained in the given clue. This means that general knowledge plays a lesser part in Complex Crosswords than in standard crosswords. By the way, watch out for the word "tea," which translates as the letter "t."

Those of you that are interested in solving standard crosswords are advised to read "How to Crack the Cryptic Crossword" by Val Gilbert, from which the above clue types are drawn.

Okay, I think you're ready to start solving now. So find a quiet place and enjoy the puzzles that follow.

POPULAR PUZZLES

SPOT THE DICE

WILLIE CRACKITT has never forgotten the puzzle that his granddad gave him as a child. The enigma consists of six regular identical dice glued together end to end in a line. Apart from the seven faces shown, the rest have no spots, the problem being to deduce the numbers on the blank faces. The top faces must use the numbers 1 to 6 once only, as should the front faces.

What are the missing numbers on the six blank faces shown?

[Hint 8; Solution 5]

The Missing Rum

O N THE BAD ship Naughty Nellie, five of the crew had been ordered to stand on deck in a line. Someone had drunk the captain's rum and the culprit was one of the five crewmen. Captain Crutch appeared and hobbled up and down the line.

"I can smell rum on yer breath, matey!" he said to the man in the middle. Big Bob was standing next to and on the right of either Cruel Colin or Evil Eddie, and Dirty Dog was two places from Awful Andrew. Exactly three consecutive places were in alphabetical order.

Who had drunk the rum?

[Hint 27; Solution 21]

THE WIZARD'S SPELL

L EGEND has it that the ruler of Salad City, Count Lettuce, had a
reputation for cruelty. He would demand unreasonable quantities
of tomatoes in tax and charge outrageous amounts of mayonnaise as
rent on his properties.

At Carrot Castle, the sorcerer was so furious about his latest rent
demand that he changed the count into a furry creature. However, better judgment soon prevailed, and he began to look in his spell book for
an incantation to restore him. The only spell that would work had four
missing letters, and they had to be inserted in the correct order:

NEED EYE OF TOAD, LEAN DOG,
LAY (4 letters) ON TRAY, LEG OF FROG.

So he placed the count on a tray and recited the spell with the missing
letters included. It worked! Time for the sorcerer to make himself disappear!

What had the count been turned into?

[Hint 5; Solution 15]

12

PACKING BOXES

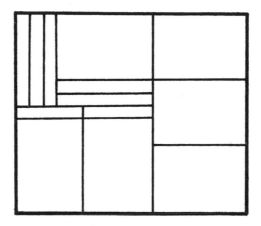

Mr. Plain was absentminded and had forgotten how many identical boxes of his finest chocolates could fill a packing case. Unfortunately, Almond, his assistant, didn't know either, so Mr. Plain ordered Almond to count the boxes. When Almond opened a packing case, he saw the rectangular view shown above, and knowing that the boxes were packed the same way to the bottom of the case with no free space, he immediately deduced the smallest number of boxes that could be inside.

What number did Almond find?

[Hint 23; Solution 34]

Cons and Conjurors

THERE was something quite unusual about the cards on the table at the Cons and Conjurors Card Club. The six card sharps at the table had each been dealt two cards, one faceup and one facedown, and each of the numbers from 1 to 12 appeared once only (where the ace is 1, the jack is 11, and the queen is 12). It all looked slightly suspicious!

The faceup cards were 2,4,5,7,10, and 11—and one of these was paired with a card three less, one with a card two less, one with a card one less, one with a card one greater, one with a card two greater, and one with a card three greater.

What number was each faceup card paired with?

[Hint 17; Solution 1]

MUMBLE MEADOW

Time	Name	Creature	Pajamas
9 A.M.	Cecil	slug	blue
10 A.M.	Bertha	wildebeest	yellow
11 A.M.	Agatha	centipede	green
12 noon	Herbert	hippopotamus	red

IF YOU WANT to find out what time certain creatures get up in the morning, the best thing to do is to go down to Mumble Meadow. That's just what Binoculars Bill did, and he scribbled the details down on his notepad as soon as he got home. Although he managed to write each item in the correct column, he managed to get only one item correctly positioned against the time in each column. What he actually observed was as follows:

At 10 A.M., either Agatha or Herbert rose, but wearing neither blue nor yellow pajamas. At the time either Cecil or Bertha rolled out of bed it was not with green pajamas, and it was not as the slug or the wildebeest. One hour later, the creature that got up had neither red nor green pajamas. Agatha did not rise at noon, and the hippopotamus rose at 9 A.M.

Can you give the name, creature, and pajamas color for each getting-up time?

[Hint 30; Solution 38]

Complex Crossword 1

OPPOSITE is a 10x10 grid of squares into which the solutions, which alternate across and down, to the cryptic clues should be inserted. The solutions are to be found in sequence and can be placed anywhere on the grid, with one letter to a square—but each new solution must overlap with some previous word(s) placed on the grid, except for the first word, which can go anywhere. On placing a new word, no non-valid words can be created from letters already on the grid.

When the ten solutions have been positioned (and there may be several ways of doing it), it should be possible to fit the extra word AXE into the word pattern, and this can be done in only one way.

The aim of the Complex Crossword is, therefore, to answer the question: Where does the AXE fall?

Clues

Across: Restrained, returned denial to Enoch, without hole (9)
Down: Actor, in royal pen, is not on (6)
Across: Islands, no dry tea in bitter day with rain (7)
Down: Sense, return to revile crepes without lucidity initially (8)
Across: Sell pie for figure (7)
Down: Writer, someone's bitter (6)
Across: Tempted, divine with tea (7)
Down: Painter, first landscapes undulated in northern Italy (5)
Across: Collar, some Bella pelting us (5)
Down: Fade, expire, at first Denis, without Rex and Peter initially (3)

[Hint 28; Solution 14]

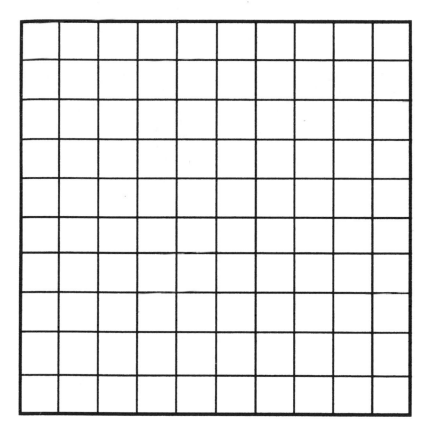

DUCK TO CAT

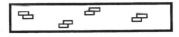

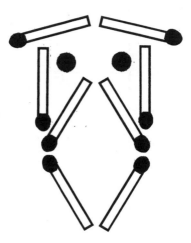

A s WHISKERS the cat was enjoying a walk one Saturday afternoon, he spied Dotty the duck in the nearby pond. Under cover of the wall at the top end of the pond, Whiskers tiptoed towards the water. He waited his moment, and when Dotty was close enough, Whiskers popped up from behind the wall and scared her away. Dotty is shown constructed from eight matches and two small coins.

Can you move exactly two matches to change the duck into a cat?

[Hint 6; Solution 16]

Cannibals

THE CHOMPEM cannibals of Drybone Island have the annoying habit of eating each other. In fact, Grandpa Chompem went missing only last week and it was thought he'd lost his way home until someone found his bits and pieces lying on the beach.

Now, one evening the Chompems threw a dinner party, one of those bring-your-own-food affairs—the invitations read "bring a friend." Six cannibals turned up, and they decided to eat each person in turn. So someone was selected for the others to eat (except the victim!), and when he had been eaten, someone else was selected, and so on. Usually, it took each cannibal on his own, two hours to eat just one person.

How long was it before just one consumer remained?

[Hint 25; Solution 18]

Paw Poem

I F TATTY stray cats only meow,
Pray let's end the error ask now:
Do uncouth toms terse,
Eat rats need our nurse,
So eight new solutions endow?

To what is this limerick referring?

[Hint 2; Solution 11]

Library Logic

A T CROTCHETY town library, seven books had been placed on a shelf in alphabetical order of title instead of alphabetical order of author. When Nasty Nora, the long-serving librarian, found out she got even nastier. She fired all the library staff and vowed never to trust anyone again (she had had a difficult childhood).

When they were correctly positioned, *Cruel Cake Recipes* was somewhere to the left of *Grandma the Pole-vaulter,* which was three places to the right of *Desert Pub Crawl. Baking a Brick* was an even number of places to the right of *Evenings in the Bath,* and *Faking a Heart Attack* was two places from *After-Dinner Insults.* Exactly three books were correctly positioned.

What was the correct order?

[Hint 42; Solution 49]

Tiny Tum's Homework

T INY TUM'S mathematics homework book was the untidiest in the class. In fact, it was so bad that Mr. Grouch, his mathematics teacher, blew a fuse. One equation that appeared in his book is shown above. The two different arithmetic signs had been erased and an x had been scribbled in place of the missing whole number x, which was the same on both sides of the equation.

What was the missing number?

[Hint 29; Solution 27]

Colored Kits

Position	Shirt	Shorts	Socks
1	purple	brown	red
2	yellow	blue	orange
3	pink	green	violet

THE FIRST three places in the Kick and Run soccer league were occupied by teams wearing different-colored football kits (outfits). The league secretary had just written down the color of the shirt, shorts, and socks for each place. Although she managed to get each color in the correct column, her mind was on Handsome Henry, who was at the next desk—so she only managed to position one color in each column correctly. Know-all Norman, the office foreman, seeing the error, decided not to divulge the correct positions but instead elected to increase his sense of importance by tormenting the secretary with some clues.

The pink was with a color beginning with B and also with either violet or orange. The shirt in first place was either a purple or a yellow one. The red was with a color beginning with P and also with either green or brown. The second place shorts were not blue.

Can you give the color of the shirt, shorts, and socks for each place?

[Hint 32; Solution 46]

Complex Crossword 2

O PPOSITE is a 10x10 grid of squares into which the solutions, which alternate across and down, to the cryptic clues should be inserted. The solutions are to be found in sequence and can be placed anywhere on the grid, with one letter to a square—but each new solution must overlap with some previous word(s) placed on the grid, except for the first word, which can go anywhere. On placing a new word, no non-valid words can be created from letters already on the grid.

When the ten solutions have been positioned (and there may be several ways of doing it), it should be possible to fit the extra word AXE into the word pattern, and this can be done in only one way.

The aim of the Complex Crossword is, therefore, to answer the question: Where does the AXE fall?

Clues

Across: Bed, returning from field archaeology (6)

Down: Mark, do try paint, not today (5)

Across: Well known, some are nought laborious without bear laugh (9)

Down: Wealthier, deer chin (8)

Across: Some whisper Isherwood, to decay (6)

Down: Scrutinize, in usual detail preventing all use (5)

Across: Chief, can ask rich doctor if natives are loaded, primarily (8)

Down: Gas, a neon lighter, doesn't heal (8)

Across: Finish, some wooden door (3)

Down: Nearby, Reg said "be in," without a grin (6)

[Hint 35; Solution 23]

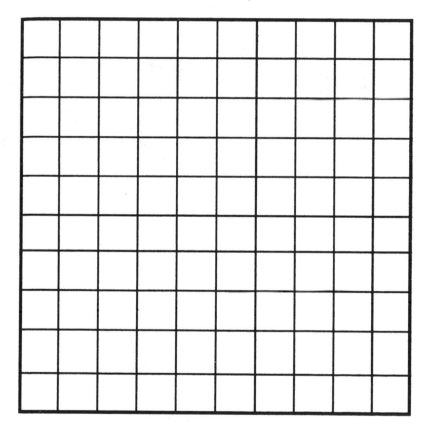

The Two Jacks

"**D**O YOU ALWAYS believe what you see?" asked Snorkel, taking four cards from a regular pack and discarding the rest. "What do you mean?" replied Twanger. Snorkel showed Twanger the four cards: an ace, a three, a ten, and a jack. After secretly arranging them in a certain order, he dealt them facedown in a line on the table. "Ah," cried Twanger, "You want me to tell you where the jack is." "*The* jack?!" exclaimed Snorkel. "There are two jacks in these four cards."

How is it possible, and where are they?

[Hint 10; Solution 7]

Fair Game

A S COLONEL BUCKSHOT twiddled his mustache nervously, the lion crouched low, ready to pounce. Buckshot raised his rifle and took aim, his finger resting on the trigger. There could be only one shot and it had to be true. The lion edged forward, still crouched low. The jungle fell silent in anticipation. Suddenly, the lion roared. Buckshot fired. When the smoke cleared, the lion was dead. The diagram shows the lion lying down, facing to the left.

Move exactly one match to kill the lion.

[Hint 33; Solution 44]

Doors to
Freedom

THE PRISONER sat alone in his cell staring through the bars at the six doors to the guardroom beyond them. Suddenly, there was the sound of footsteps. One guard came in through door A, and a second entered through door F. They unlocked the cell door.

"We will set you free," said one of the guards, "but first you must pass through all six doors, each door once only, in the correct order. Three are exits only, and three are entrances only. Door A must be followed by door B or E, B by C or E, C by D or F, D by A or F, E by B or D, and F by C or D." With that, the guards left through door B.

In what order must the prisoner pass through the doors?

[Hint 3; Solution 2]

Deleting Sheep

3	8	6	7	5	3	4	5
7	5	4	3	9	5	9	2
5	3	9	6	1	4	8	6
8	5	2	5	4	6	5	9
1	3	5	8	5	7	4	6
8	7	1	6	9	6	5	1
4	7	9	7	2	3	5	4
6	4	5	1	9	8	3	8

"WANT ANY of them there sheep?" said Farmer Jowls to a prospective buyer at the livestock market. The buyer surveyed the flock, which were secured in sixty-four pens arranged in a 8x8 square grid, the number in each pen being shown above. "I want to make a tidy sum out of it," said the farmer. So, in line with the farmer's wish, the buyer bought all the sheep in sixteen of the pens.

Delete two numbers in each row so that each horizontal and vertical line totals 30.

[Hint 16; Solution 25]

Fantasy Island

Position	Chappie	Lassie	House Name
1	Wally the Wizard	Sugar Plum Fairy	Cobbler's Castle
2	Pixie Nose	Matilda the Witch	Dungblock Dungeon
3	Good Elf	Doris the Mermaid	Paradise Palace
4	Happy Herman	Wicked Queen	Vegetable Patch

ON FANTASY ISLAND, the results of the Happy Household competition had just been printed in the local newspaper, with a chappie, lassie, and house name for each entry. Each item appeared in the correct column, but unfortunately, due to a printer's error, only one entry in each column was correctly positioned.

It turned out that second place went to Wally the Wizard, who lived at neither Dungblock Dungeon nor the Vegetable Patch, and not with Doris the Mermaid. Just after him was neither Pixie Nose nor Happy Herman—but whoever it was, he lived at Cobbler's Castle with either the Sugar Plum Fairy or the Wicked Queen. Either Doris the Mermaid or Matilda the Witch lived at either Cobbler's Castle or Dungblock Dungeon.

Can you give the correct chappie, lassie, and house name for each position?

[Hint 34; Solution 35]

BYE BYE ALIBI

W HEN SID BONE was murdered in a rather compromising position, Inspector Twiggit suspected Sid's wife Nora. Nora, however, steadfastly maintained that on the evening of the murder, she was in a restaurant with a man friend. Twiggit had found an entry in Nora's diary for that evening which apparently confirmed her alibi as follows: TIPS THE BRUSHED CHEFS. However, Twiggit realized that the message was coded and that each letter could be moved either one place forwards or one place backwards in the alphabet to reveal a startling confession.

What was the hidden confession?

[Hint 9; Solution 6]

Complex Crossword 3

O PPOSITE is a 10x10 grid of squares into which the solutions, which alternate across and down, to the cryptic clues should be inserted. The solutions are to be found in sequence and can be placed anywhere on the grid, with one letter to a square—but each new solution must overlap with some previous word(s) placed on the grid, except for the first word, which can go anywhere. On placing a new word, no non-valid words can be created from letters already on the grid.

When the ten solutions have been positioned (and there may be several ways of doing it), it should be possible to fit the extra word AXE into the word pattern, and this can be done in only one way.

The aim of the Complex Crossword is, therefore, to answer the question: Where does the AXE fall?

Clues

Across: Shows pressure, back from more temporary business, don't pry (9)

Down: Fragment, in lice trap (8)

Across: Steam, can launder oily underwear, dirty socks ... that's just the beginning! (6)

Down: Temperamental, returning from scary doom (5)

Across: Boats, coy star has, without oars (6)

Down: Disinterested, returns with modern object, no novelty at first (7)

Across: Dress, some fur object, without jacket initially (4)

Down: Towards, forefront of alternative technology (2)

Across: Unwell, General Reilly lacks real energy (3)

Down: Yield, in morose internment cell, no comment lone sir (6)

[Hint 39; Solution 28]

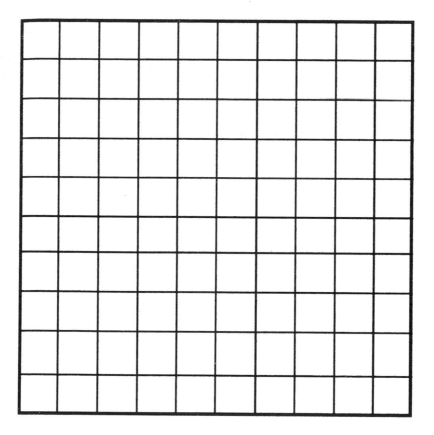

The Stolen Sweets

THE TWO Gobler twins each had a bag of sweets.

"I've got more sweets than you," said Mollusc with a hint of superiority.

"So give me some, then," replied Tweaker, and from the bag Mollusc was holding he grabbed a number of sweets equal to one third of the number of sweets he already had and threw them in his own bag.

"Look!" shouted Mollusc. "There's a dinosaur under the table!"

As Tweaker turned to look, Mollusc retrieved all the stolen sweets from Tweaker's bag, a number equal to one third of the number remaining in his bag, and returned them to his own bag. Altogether the twins had 35 sweets.

How many sweets does each twin have?

[Hint 26; Solution 20]

Round the Table

A T THE ANNUAL dinner of the Whisky Bottle-top Collectors Club, the six members were sitting around a circular table. As the whisky flowed, inhibitions were forgotten. Insults flowed, too, and each diner started to fight with his two neighbors.

Throgmorton was so incensed about Delilah's criticism of his flowered tie that he "accidentally" spilt his drink over her dress. When Horace objected, Throgmorton threw his toupee in his soup. Arbuthnot was telling rude Irish jokes which, since Gertrude was Irish, was ill advised, and she promptly planted his face in his sponge and custard. Prigwick propelled his own sponge and custard in Arbuthnot's direction.

By this time, Horace had launched into his "Britain was great when it had an empire" speech, and Gertrude decided that since donkeys like carrots, she could do no better than place one up his left nostril.

Luckily, each person got on well with the other three (except for Prigwick who didn't get on with Horace).

What is the only seating arrangement (clockwise or counterclockwise) for arguments to be avoided?

[Hint 37; Solution 42]

Cups and Balls

G ISYERLOOT FAIR had arrived in town. "Roll up! Roll up!" shouted one stall owner. "A prize for guessing the number of balls under the cups!"

On the counter in front of him were four upturned cups. Each concealed the same number of balls. On each cup was a statement about the number of balls underneath. From left to right they read as follows.

"One or four," "two or four," "two or three," or "one or two." Only one of the four statements was correct.

How many balls were under a cup and which statement was true?

[Hint 13; Solution 10]

THE TORN MESSAGE

A S SLIPPERY SAM, the notorious villain, sipped his tenth beer in the Pig and Bucket, special agent Larry the Lurker was keeping surveillance. Larry had been following Sam for days, patiently waiting for him to leave rendezvous instructions for his contact. So far, nothing.

Suddenly, Sam, boozed to the brim, staggered out of the bar. A torn-up square of paper had been left next to his empty glass and the pieces had letters scribbled on them. This must be it! Larry rushed to the bar and quickly assembled the pieces to make the message shown; however, it was not what Larry expected. Larry had been led to believe that the rendezvous was at a ladies' party at a health retreat. There is only one other way to assemble the pieces to make a meaningful message.

What is the message?

[Hint 7; Solution 3]

Cubic Hexagon

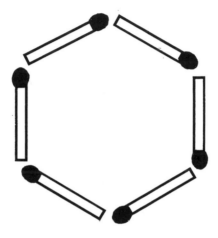

Down at the Pig and Bucket, the regulars were enjoying their usual drinking binge. Burper took six matches and laid them out in the form of the regular hexagon shown.

"Right," said Burper. "All you have to do is add just two matches to change this hexagon into a cube."

Legless was convinced that double vision was needed to see the answer, so he ordered another pint. However, it was no trick question. With the matches correctly added, a view of a cube appeared.

How is it possible?

[Hint 11; Solution 33]

Untying the Knot

Time	Groom Names First Second		Bride Names First Second		Room
10 A.M.	Danny	Popple	Irma	Peebles	Cupid
11 A.M.	Arnold	Witless	Jenny	Fiddle	Royal
12 noon	Colin	Hogwash	Karen	Boggle	Happy
1 P.M.	Bernie	Rumble	Lorna	Grumble	Smoochy

A T RUBBLE Registry Office, the ceremonies booked for the day were listed as above. Mrs. Wonsell, the administrator, had written each item in the correct column but only one item in each column was correctly positioned against the time. The couples arrived, and a fierce debate raged as to who was to be married when and where.

Mr. Rumble was in the Cupid room with neither Irma nor Jenny. Miss Grumble, who was not marrying Colin, was getting married sometime after the couple in the Smoochy room. Mr. Popple was getting married at noon, but not in the Smoochy nor Royal room. The groom being married at 1 P.M. was neither Danny nor Colin, the latter not being married at 10 A.M. either. Danny was being married to Miss Boggle one hour after Irma, who was not in the Smoochy room.

Can you rearrange the list above to give the time, full names, and room for each couple?

[Hint 40; Solution 50]

Complex
Crossword 4

OPPOSITE is a 10x10 grid of squares into which the solutions, which alternate across and down, to the cryptic clues should be inserted. The solutions are to be found in sequence and can be placed anywhere on the grid, with one letter to a square—but each new solution must overlap with some previous word(s) placed on the grid, except for the first word, which can go anywhere. On placing a new word, no non-valid words can be created from letters already on the grid.

When the ten solutions have been positioned (and there may be several ways of doing it), it should be possible to fit the extra word AXE into the word pattern, and this can be done in only one way.

The aim of the Complex Crossword is, therefore, to answer the question: Where does the AXE fall?

Clues

Across: Widow, some robber eavesdropping (7)
Down: Compound, ice bread not eaten at first (7)
Across: Animate, ripe sin (7)
Down: Show up, with Robert initially, returning gross Arab meals (9)
Across: Drink, real without Rachel (3)
Down: Steam, turned our pavement upside down (6)
Across: Stern oarsman, takes whore, without awe, no help at first (6)
Down: 'e did not, see rise, to succession (6)
Across: Communist, reads no Alexander Solzhenitsyn at first (3)
Down: Sense organ, some heard (3)

[Hint 43; Solution 40]

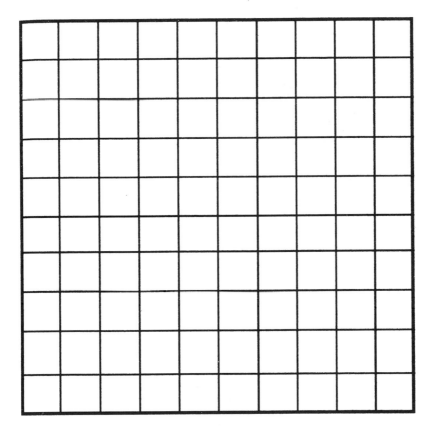

Square Words

R	A	N	T
R	I	F	E
D	A	M	E
T	I	M	E

TODDLER TOBY had been playing with his lettered building bricks on the floor. "Look!" he shouted excitedly. He had arranged sixteen of his bricks into a 4x4 grid to make the words RANT, RIFE, DAME, and TIME reading across the rows. Unfortunately, only the dog Scratter was in the room, and he had no intention of leaving his bone to look at a few blocks of wood.

"But watch this!" cried Toby. Scratter retreated to the garden with his bone. Meanwhile Toby had rearranged the sixteen bricks to make four different words, which read the same across the rows as down the columns.

What were the four words?

[Hint 38; Solution 29]

Truth and Treasure

I SMELL A RAT.

SCATTERBRAIN, the treasurer, was a bit of a . . . well, scatterbrain, and had forgotten how many gold, silver, and bronze coins were kept in the town vaults. Rather than spend the rest of his life counting them out, he decided to ask the three guards, each of whom guarded one type of coin, how many coins were in his charge. The guards were the uncooperative sort, and the best that Scatterbrain could get from each one was a statement about the numbers of coins in the other two vaults.

Dimwit, who was guarding the gold, said there were 3,000 silver and 5,000 bronze coins; Thickplank, who was in charge of the silver, said there were 3,000 gold and 5,000 bronze coins; and Beefbrain, who was protecting the bronze, said there were 4,000 gold and 3,000 silver coins. To make matters worse, only one guard was being truthful, each of the other two stating at least one false amount.

If there were 12,000 coins in total, how many of each type were there?

[Hint 31; Solution 45]

Parking Space

Position	Captain	Species	Spaceship	Planet
1.	Dib	Monopips	Geegeepuld	Blip
2.	Wop	Babbles	Outagas	Delta
3.	Fud	Dinoblobs	Boldleego	Vulcan
4.	Jim	Fiddlypoos	Runsoncole	Luminus

O N PLANET Sigma V, the First Galactic Spacepeople Convention was underway. A representative from each technologically advanced planet in the galaxy was present; however, when it came to deciding the priority for spaceship parking spaces, there was a such a heated row that laser guns were drawn. The problem was that the convention organizer had written down the list shown above—and although he had each item in the correct column, only one item in each column was correctly positioned. However, the following facts were certain:

Either the Babble or Dinoblob was first, but neither Boldleego nor Outagas was second. The spaceship from Delta was either Boldleego or Outagas, but was captained by neither Dib nor Jim. A Babble was not third, and the Babble that captained Outagas was either Dib or Jim. Wop was from neither Blip nor Vulcan and was neither a Babble nor a Dinoblob. The captain in fourth place was either from Blip or Vulcan.

Can you find the captain, species, spaceship, and planet for each parking position?

[Hint 45; Solution 51]

TEASER TALES

The Torque Wrench

"**Y**OU GOT the torque wrench?" asked Fred.

"Don't talk to me about the torque wrench," said Bob. "It's been days since I've seen it."

In fact, no one at Greasegun Garage had seen the torque wrench for weeks. "If you ask me," said the foreman, "I think a customer took it by mistake. Come on, let's look in the log book."

So they thumbed through the list of customers in the log book until they reached entries around the time it disappeared.

"Why don't you go and visit them?" said the foreman. So Fred had a quick wash to remove the oil on his hands, climbed on his bicycle, and set off.

At 7 Ludwig Lane, Fred found a large man weeding his front garden. Why he'd want to do that when it was all concrete, Fred had no idea. Anyway, he came to a stop just outside the gate at number 7.

"Excuse me," said Fred politely. The weeder raised his large frame to its full six feet five inches. "Er, you remember me?" began Fred. "You brought your car in a few weeks ago."

"That's right," said the weeder. Recognition! Now Fred could relax. "Trouble is," said the weeder, "It ain't worked since." Fred's confidence crumbled. The weeder put down his trowel. "Anyway, what can I do for you?" "Well," said Fred. "I was wondering if you'd seen our torque wrench." The weeder ran his fingernails through the bristles on his chin, cleared his throat with a loud chesty cough, then pointed towards the front door, which was wide open. "My son in there, if you take twice the age he was six years ago, you'll get three times the age he was ten years ago."

Fred wondered how that could be important. Maybe his son's age stood for some letter, the position of that letter in the alphabet. But before he could enquire, the weeder had gone. Fred cycled on his way.

At 12 Pooper Place, he pressed the bell on the front door and waited. Nothing. So he pressed it again. Suddenly, the door flew open and before him . . . was a man juggling four pieces of fruit! An apple, banana, pear, and orange!

"Yes?"

"Er, I'm looking for the torque wrench, you know, from the garage. You brought your car in a while back."

"Torque wrench," said the juggler, then spun a full circle on the spot, keeping all four fruits in the air. "The apple says the pear or banana's got it, the banana says the apple or orange has it, the orange says it's the apple or banana, and the pear says it's him or the banana. But you know what fruits are like, only one of them's telling the truth." Fred couldn't believe he was hearing this. "I'm working up to five fruits," said the juggler. "Fruit cocktail it's called."

Fred was thinking more along the lines of fruitcake. He thought he'd better leave quickly, in case it was contagious. Why would pieces of fruit need a torque wrench? Perhaps, reasoned Fred, the culprit among the juggler's fruit was a clue. Maybe it was the first letter of that fruit that he needed.

At 49 Little Side, Fred could get no answer whatsoever, no matter how hard he pressed the bell or knocked the knocker. He peered through the window. No one in. On a sign next to the front door was the house name "Spoke." How curious. And what was he to make of the sign on the door that said "Go to the front." He *was* at the front. He knew he was looking for a single letter, that's how it had worked at the last two houses, but what clues were there as to what it was? Mmm . . . four, nine, little, side, spoke, and "Go to the front." What this some kind of instruction about the missing letter? He'd have to think about that one.

At the next house on his list, he was met at the door by a very large woman in an apron. "Mrs. Trumpet at your service. Catering for all occasions. Parties, weddings, birthdays . . . chocolate cakes, cream cakes, currant cakes . . . bread rolls, sausage rolls. . . ."

Fred thought it better to stop her before he was persuaded to buy something. He explained his predicament.

"Well," said Mrs. Trumpet. "I'll give you something to think about. The washing-up's in with the price. But do you know who can *clean the pans* (9,3)?"

Fred didn't know. But if this was a clue and he was after a single letter, then he thought he'd better take the first letter of whatever she was talking about.

It was the final house on Fred's list. One more letter to go. Just as Fred entered the driveway the postman appeared from seemingly nowhere and threw some envelopes onto the front lawn. They fell in a neat line.

"For you," said the postman.

"But I don't live here," said Fred.

"Still for you," said the postman. "Eight letters. First one's from Fiona or Ian, who are three places from each other; Mark's is some place before Karen's, Harry's is three places from Lorna's. . . ."

"Wait!" said Fred, holding up his hand. "Why are you telling me all this?"

"Dunno," said the postman. "Oh yes, Karen's is not next to Lorna's or Harry's, and June's is four places from George's."

Fred stooped to pick them up.

"Wait!" cried the postman. "Just kidding. Actually, only the last letter's for you."

Fred now had five letters from his visits to help his investigation. Needless to say, the correct arrangement of the five will answer the mystery of what happened to the torque wrench!

[Solution 39]

Seven Secrets

THE YOUTHFUL Manichop had won many battles of the mind. Sought by kings and emperors throughout the ancient lands, his mental powers could dissect the most intricate of enigmas.

It was said that Manichop had descended from Wolklan, the Power of Wisdom, who had held the Seven Secrets of the Evil Cave where Yants, the Power of Darkness, lived. These secrets had given Wolklan the power to stop Yants and his evil deeds. Unfortunately, Wolklan had been slain by Yants, who had taken on the form of a poisonous snake to gain entry to Wolklan's castle. Once the secrets had died with Wolklan, Yants had been left with unlimited power which he used to terrorize the people, sending hurricanes, plagues, and droughts. The rulers of all the ancient lands had finally decided that Yants must be stopped, and only one person could do it.

Manichop stood before the entrance to the Evil Cave where Yants lived, his long blond hair flowing in the breeze, his deep brown eyes reaching out into the darkness within. High on the Mountain of Death a storm picked up and, in a gesture of unwelcome, tossed Manichop's green cloak into the valley below. Inside the cave, enigmas waited to be solved. If Manichop could pass all the tests on his journey through the cave and thereby discover the Seven Secrets, Yants would be defeated.

Manichop stepped into the cave. Foul rotten smells filled his nostrils, piercing screams attacked his ears, and haunting visions of pain and torture flashed out of the darkness before him. Yants was tormenting him. Manichop continued. He remembered the ancient scroll found in Wolklan's castle after his death that gave clues to the Seven Secrets of the Evil Cave.

> Seven Secrets surely fall,
> Wit and wisdom solve them all,
> Sometimes one unlocks the next,
> Sometimes not, but be not vexed,
> First of each take to the last,
> The dragon's fire, will get you past.

The First Secret

Suddenly, a river of gold appeared, with a bridge across it. Five dwarfs were standing by the bridge discussing the order they should cross.

"Me and you are going one straight after the other," said Asp to Ether.

"I'm going two places after you," said Heathen to Reaper.

"I'm going three places before you," said Ether to Torrent.

With that, the dwarfs passed over the bridge one at a time. As Manichop crossed the bridge, he realized they had vanished. What was the significance of their order, he wondered.

The Second Secret

He had no time to think about it. A ball of fire burst in front of him. The intensity of the heat made Manichop recoil, his arms covering his face. He heard laughter reverberate around the chamber. Yants was enjoying Manichop's pain. As Manichop stepped back he stumbled over something on the ground. He looked down to see bricks, soil, water, bellows, and cloak. One of them must put out the fire. Manichop chose correctly because the fireball subsided leaving the path ahead clear. Manichop wiped the sweat from his forehead and walked on.

The Third Secret

It was dark and silent. Manichop felt completely alone. His only sensation was the rocky ground beneath his bare feet. As he pressed one foot after the other into the sand, sharp stones began to pierce his flesh. The pain rose up through his body like a hot blade flashing from within. He clenched his fists and gritted his teeth. He must continue.

There was no way back. Then the pain vanished.

"Do you want to know my dreams?" said a voice.

A pale light from the roof enveloped the figure of a frail old man sitting cross-legged on the ground. A ragged brown cape barely covered him.

"Dreams?" enquired Manichop with some surprise.

"Let me tell you what I dream of," said the old the man. "Insect, heroic day, dried grass, expanse of water. If you order them (a), (b), (c), (d), which would you place first?"

"Well, I'm not sure," replied Manichop. "How important are they to *you?*"

There was no reply. The old man had gone. It was an interesting problem. How was it possible to rank them. Surely it was a subjective matter—or was it?

The Fourth Secret

"Fight, you coward!" bellowed a voice. As Manichop turned to his left, he saw a giant, a heavy steel sword clasped in his iron fist. He was certainly a powerful figure. Over four meters tall, his gigantic torso carried steel armor plating held in place by strong padlocks. His legs were wrapped in heavy chains that no sword could penetrate. Spiked lead boots protected his feet and offered a fatal kick to anyone who ventured close enough. He was not a man Manichop wanted to engage in combat. Suddenly, Manichop saw a goose, a warrior, a horse, and a crocodile close by to the right. Perhaps he could offer the giant a goose as a gift to let him pass, or the warrior could fight the giant on his behalf. Or Manichop could gallop past on the horse, or the crocodile could topple the giant with his powerful teeth. Whichever one he picked, it would need to be bribed in order to cooperate. Manichop thought for a moment then chose. The giant faded away.

The Fifth Secret

The temperature was dropping. Manichop began to shiver. He realized that he must complete the remaining tasks soon or freeze to death in the cave. He guessed that Yants was angry with his success and had decided to set time against him to hurry him into error.

A ravine appeared in the distance. Manichop ran towards it. It was about 10 meters wide and 3 meters deep, with hissing cobras lying in wait at the bottom. Manichop wrapped his arms around his chest as a biting wind encircled him. There was little time left. There had to be a way across.

Suddenly, a fluttering of wings filled the air, and over the ravine came a giant eagle. "I am Grandeous," screeched the eagle as he circled above Manichop.

Then, in a gigantic leap, a gazelle bounded across the ravine. "I am Nentarl," whispered the gazelle as he ground to a halt next to Manichop.

Following the gazelle flew a winged tiger. "I am Souvici," snarled the tiger, as he raced past.

"And I am Pulefist!" It was a boa constrictor that had stretched out across the ravine forming a bridge.

It all seemed like a trick by Yants. There was no apparent way of choosing the correct one to pass over the ravine. Manichop fell to his knees as the frost embraced him like a cruel friend. He prepared himself for a freezing death. Yants had outwitted him, just as he had outwitted Wolklan his ancestor. Now the ancient lands were destined for another thousand years of terror.

In a final act of desperation, Manichop gazed across the ravine. What he saw saved his life. He unraveled the fifth secret to cross the ravine.

The Sixth Secret
On the other side was a tunnel that led to the cave exit. At the entrance to the tunnel he found a map, illumination, headgear, and a knife. Manichop chose just one and entered the tunnel. He knew that his choice had been sound, because soon he saw the sunlight that rushed in through the cave exit. He had completed six tasks and now the final task awaited him.

The Seventh Secret
As Manichop moved towards the exit, the temperature rose swiftly and he soon found himself facing a fire-breathing dragon blocking his path to freedom. If Manichop was to be triumphant he would need all the powers of thought at his disposal. What did he need to pass the dragon? What was it that the scroll said?

Manichop reached the outside world where he was much praised by the rulers of the ancient lands. Yants died a broken spirit soon afterwards, and the power of evil died with him. The Seven Secrets of the Evil Cave that Manichop had discovered elevated him to the Power of Wisdom, a position that Wolkan had once held. The people of the ancient lands could now live in peace.

What are the seven secrets?

[Solution 32]

The Missing Sandwiches

M R. GLOOMBY was pacing up and down his office like a man possessed. It was a bad morning; he'd lost the keys to the drinks cabinet, his telephone was out of order and now . . . Gloomby hit the intercom button. "I'd like to have Miss Flaunt in my office right away."

He sank into his chair with his head in his hands. Miss Flaunt, his personal assistant, came in and smiled seductively as her trim figure glided across the room. "You said you'd like to have me in your office," she said, undoing the top button of her blouse.

Gloomby was clearly embarrassed. "Yes, er . . . no, er, it's my cash box! It's gone missing!"

"Missing?"

"Yes, Missing! M-I-S . . . er, missing!"

"What was in it?" asked Miss Flaunt seriously.

"My sandwiches, that's what! And I want everyone in here now!"

Miss Flaunt turned for the door. Her dress sense was often a talking point. In fact, at the office party her brown skirt with yellow polka dots was likened to an unbuttered crumpet. Several people felt like toasting it.

Ten minutes later, the office staff were in Gloomby's office. There was Mrs. Bucket the cleaning lady, Mrs. O'Hara from switchboard, Mr. Ogden the plumber, Mr. Panic from security, Mr. Scrooge the accountant, Mr. Rossi the buyer, and Miss Nib the secretary.

"Right!" said Gloomby. "My cash box has gone missing and with it, two slices of ham and cucumber that my wife made only this morning. I want to know the order that you all arrived this morning."

It was the first time they'd seen Gloomby so angry—since yesterday, at any rate—and it was not a pleasant sight. His eyes were red with rage, his nostrils flared, and Mrs. O'Hara swore she could see steam coming out of his ears. Even the rubber plant stood to attention. Mr. Scrooge, the accountant, calculated that it was just about safe enough to speak.

"Er, I know I was in sometime after Mr. Rossi."

"And I came in either straight before or straight after Miss Nib," piped up O'Hara.

"Mrs. Bucket always comes in either two places before or after me," said Ogden, gaining in confidence.

Gloomby nodded knowingly. It was quite a tense moment. One had the feeling that the next person to speak might be terminally savaged.

"I'm always three places before Mr. Rossi," said Panic from security, with a smile that probably saved him. Panic was an odd choice for security. A reformed kleptomaniac, he was as thin as a greyhound and always hid in the cupboard every time the fire alarm went off.

But did Gloomby think that someone had stolen his sandwiches? Surely that was ridiculous. Miss Nib was the one who raised the matter.

"Er, I'm never more than two places before or after Mr. Ogden. But Mr. Gloomby, surely you don't think someone stole your sandwiches?"

"Stole them?!" exclaimed Gloomby with a laugh. "Of course not! I just want to know where they are, and I think the last one of you can tell me that."

Assuming that the seven arrived consecutively, what was their order and where were the sandwiches?

[Solution 47]

Autumn Acres

A S THE SUN rose over Autumn Acres, the field began to awaken. Squeaker the mouse emerged from his home beneath the tree trunk, realized that he still had his nightcap on, then scrambled back inside again before anyone noticed. Hoppity the rabbit darted across the field in merry little leaps, stopping for a moment to nibble a lettuce. Spike the hedgehog, on his way home from a good night's forage, rummaged through a pile of leaves hoping to find an insect. Meanwhile, across the field on the old wooden gate sat Wise Owl, calmly surveying all before him.

By the horse trough, Melody the sparrow was distraught. Wise Owl flew across to join her.

"My nest," said Melody, "I can't remember where it is. Every morning I go looking for food and on the way back I visit exactly six trees in a certain order so that I can remember where my nest is."

Melody dried her eyes with a leaf. Before Wise Owl could ask how the trees helped her to remember, Blackie the crow lowered her undercarriage and landed next to them. Wise Owl explained the problem.

"Well I can tell you what one of the trees is," said Blackie confidently. Unfortunately, Blackie chose the wrong time to go blank. "Er, well, I *should* know because I live next to it. I know it's a willow, oak, sycamore, or fir. Now let me see. If it's not the oak, then it's either the sycamore or the fir. If it's not the willow, then it's either the oak or the sycamore. If it's not the sycamore, then it's either the willow or the fir. And if it's not the fir, then it's either the sycamore or the oak."

Suddenly, a black pointed nose popped out of the ground.

"Nice morning," said Burrows the mole, brushing the soil off his head. Wise Owl explained why the converse was true.

"Well I know how you can find out one of the trees," said Burrows. "See the farmer's house over there? Take his tangy lemon gin without saying nothing. (3)"

"That's cryptic, isn't it?" asked Wise Owl.

Too late. Burrows had burrowed.

"I know" said Wise Owl. "Let's go and find Timid the squirrel."

On the other side of the field, Squeaker the mouse re-emerged from his house minus nightcap.

"Oh, it must have rained last night" said Squeaker to himself, noticing a small puddle outside his door. He bent over to look at his reflection in it.

"There's no doubt about it. You're a handsome mouse. Strong pointed nose, large straight ears and . . . Oh, no! . . . I've still got my pajamas on!" And in a fit of embarrassment, Squeaker dived back inside.

Timid the squirrel was busy hiding nuts when Melody and Wise Owl arrived. They told Timid the problem.

"I visit the same four trees in order every morning, and I nearly always see Melody on the first tree. Let me see. Either the pine, larch, or ash is first; either the pine, larch, or ash is second; either the birch or ash is third; and either the pine or birch is fourth. Oh, and I visit the pine and the ash one after the other."

Wise Owl thanked the squirrel and nudged Melody in the direction of a pile of leaves.

"What good are leaves?" asked Melody.

"What good are leaves?" said a voice indignantly. Spike the hedgehog crawled out from under them. "Best place to find insects, that's what!"

Wise Owl was ready to proceed with caution, as he knew Spike could be a bit prickly at times. But after he had told Spike about a big pile of leaves at the farmer's house, Spike was more than happy to help.

"Down by the river are five trees in a row: an oak, willow, cedar, apple, and pine, but I'm not sure about their order. I know that the willow is two away from the apple; the cedar is somewhere to the right of the oak; and the oak is next to the pine. I always see the sparrow on the tree second from the right."

Hoppity the rabbit had been listening. "Melody always visits a tree near my house in the morning," said Hoppity.

"That's right," said Melody. "Bert the beetle runs a cafe there, and I always stop for a tea. Mmm, that's useful."

They thanked their friends and set off for Squeaker's house. At the tree trunk, Squeaker was sitting outside with a napkin on his lap, nibbling a piece of mild cheddar. Melody and Wise Owl landed by his front door.

"Want some cheese?" asked Squeaker.

Wise Owl was not particularly fond of cheese, especially cheese with teeth marks in it, so he politely declined. Squeaker was briefly briefed. The mouse brought out his diary which had a table written in it.

time	friend	location	tree
9 A.M.	Weeny	viaduct	ash
10 A.M.	Meryl	barn	elm
11 A.M.	Tipsey	pond	oak

"These are the friends that I visit every morning," said Squeaker. "My diary needs a few alterations. I know each item is in the correct column but I only managed to get one item correctly positioned against the time in each column. Anyway, I know I visit either Meryl or Tipsey at 9 A.M. at either the ash or the elm. Weeny lives by either the viaduct or the pond near either the ash or the elm. At 10 A.M. I visit the barn or the viaduct. Meryl lives at the elm by either the pond or the barn. I always see Melody at 10 A.M."

Melody and Wise Owl conferred for quite some time. Then Melody's face lit up as she suddenly realized that she had all six solutions. They thanked Squeaker and turned to leave.

"Oh, by the way," said Wise Owl.

"Yes?" said the mouse.

"You've still got your bed socks on!"

Where was the sparrow's nest?

[Solution 8]

The Codfish Kung Fuer

M<small>R.</small> P<small>RESSUP</small>, the physical education teacher at Codfish Comprehensive School, had arranged for some of his pupils to see a kung fu film. Unfortunately, the boy sitting to the left of Walter the Wailer had got carried away and kung-fued Walter in the ear. Walter wailed the house down. When Pressup found out, he was so incensed that he vowed to find the culprit by inquiry and deduction. The only fact he was sure of was that the sixteen children had sat in a 4x4 square of seats in four rows and four columns.

It was Saturday morning, and Pressup began his mission. He rang the bell of the Scrubbit household and waited. A dog barked, and a rather plump unshaven fellow in a grubby vest swung open the door.

"Whad'ya want?" Pressup wondered if he'd just climbed out of a dustbin.

"Er, I'd like to speak to young Flicker."

The vest eyed him up and down suspiciously. "He ain't in. You a fed?"

"P.E. teacher."

The vest turned to the hallway. "Oy! Get yer ass over 'ere!"

Flicker appeared in the hallway, stuffing the remains of some toast in his face. Pressup was in quickly. "Friday night. Who were you sitting with?"

Unfortunately, cooperation was not Flicker's forte. "Well, at the time, Moron said he was directly to the right of Hogweed. I reckon I was directly in front of Moron. Hogweed said he was two to the right of me. Pits said he was two to the right of Hogweed. But you know what kids are nowadays. Exactly one of us was lying."

"And what about Crabtree?"

"Well, at the time, Dibdib said he was one in front of and one to the left of Crabtree. Stinker said he was one below and one to the right of Worm. Worm said he was two to the right of Crabtree. And Crabtree said he was one to the right of Worm. But you know what kids are nowadays. . . ."

Pressup sensed he had heard the rest somewhere before. "Exactly one of them was lying?"

"Yeah," said Flicker surprised.

"Now if you don't mind," said the vest, "it's time to take the gold-fish for a walk." The door slammed shut. The dog barked again as Pressup ground his teeth. If only he could have just one hour with the vest in the gym . . .

At 13 Tattered Close, Pressup rang the bell. A young lady in minimum attire peeped tentatively through the upstairs curtains. A much older man peered over her shoulder, then opened the window, laughing nervously.

"It's okay. I thought you were the wife."

"I'm looking for Squiggle Junior," said Pressup.

Suddenly the door opened and there stood Squiggle Junior, completely absorbed in a hand-held shoot-em-up. "Wicked! I've just reached ten thousand!"

Pressup waited for the lad to return to Earth, then began his inquiry.

"I reckon," said Squiggle Junior, "that if Wipsey was sitting directly behind me then I wasn't at the front of our square. But if Wipsey was directly in front of me, then I wasn't at the back of it. Either way, Stutter was two places behind Wipsey. Get my drift?"

Pressup wasn't sure he wanted it. Ah, who was this then? It was Babble on a broken bike delivering his morning round. Now, this could be useful.

"Stop right there!," shouted Pressup. "Friday evening!"

Babble braked briskly, and the wreck responded by plopping him into a puddle that the overnight downpour had deposited. As Babble bleated balefully, Pressup pounced.

"Where were you sitting?"

"Two away from Herman in the same row," replied Babble, wringing himself out. "But not at the end."

"And Polyp?"

"Polyp? Somewhere to the right of and in front of Flapper. Look! I'm soaking wet, sir!"

Pressup didn't hear. He now knew enough to discover who the Codfish kung fuer was.

Where did everyone sit and who was the culprit?

[Solution 24]

ADVANCED PUZZLES

Breaking the Circuit

S PARKY the electrician had made some lighting to brighten his evenings. The apparatus consisted of sixteen batteries labeled A–D and eight ten-volt bulbs mounted on a board. Each letter A–D represented a single-digit nonzero number of volts, though not necessarily four different values. A switch determined whether or not the circuits ran horizontally or vertically, so that each row or column of four batteries fully lit the bulb at the end of that row or column. This meant that when the batteries were correctly positioned either the column or row of bulbs could be illuminated.

As an exercise, Plug, the apprentice, had been instructed to remove all the batteries and use just three of them to fully illuminate each bulb in turn. Unfortunately, he had replaced the sixteen incorrectly (as shown) so that at least one bulb would blow both vertically and horizontally when connected. Luckily, Sparky was quite switched on and realized that he could rectify the situation by simply interchanging two batteries.

If no batteries were connected in opposition, what are the values of A,B,C, and D?

[Hint 20; Solution 22]

The Logic Cards

A	B	C
All statements with at least one card to the left are true	**All** statements next to this one are true	No statement at an end of line is true

PROFESSOR GALLOP was interviewing a prospective candidate for the School of Logic. "If you want to get into our School of Logic," he said, "you've got to be pretty smart."

"Well, I know I'm pretty," said Miss Eager.

"Ah!" Gallop interjected. "But how smart are you? You can't get through the door unless you're a genius. Even our cleaning lady has an IQ of 200."

"Well . . ."

"Look," said Gallop. "Here are three logic cards. Each one bears a statement that is either true or false. You have to position them correctly in a straight line so that there are no contradictions. Solve it and you're in."

In what order should the cards be placed and which statements are true?

[Hint 46; Solution 37]

Synchronizing Watches

A S SAD SALLY passes the town-hall clock each day at noon, she looks at the clock and changes her watch to 12:00:00 (hours:minutes:seconds). Sally then goes home, and for want of something better to do, listens for the clock chimes. She believes that the single chime she hears at regular intervals occurs each hour on the hour, and since her watch is always wrong, she alters it accordingly. In reality, her watch runs at the same rate as the town-hall clock, but the clock chimes whenever the minute and hour hands point in the same direction.

What time is on Sally's watch (to the nearest minute) when she passes the town-hall clock?

[Hint 24; Solution 26]

THE
SIX DIGITS

$$\boxed{} + \boxed{} = \boxed{}$$

IT WAS puzzle time down the Pig and Bucket. "It's a real digital dilemma," remarked Bert as he sipped his ale. Alf had the self-satisfied smile he always wore when he was confident that he had Bert over a barrel. Alf had drawn the boxes above on a card and given Bert the digits 1–6. Bert had to put two digits in each box, using each digit once and once only, to make a valid equation.

Without introducing further symbols, how can it be done?

[Hint 22; Solution 31]

Old Automobiles

A T GOBLIN GARAGE, the cars were having a discussion about their ages.

"You must both be the same age," said Banger. "And I must be younger than both of you."

"How come?" enquired Tooter.

"You've both got four tires and I've only got three."

Tooter looked at Hooter with a sigh. There was no doubt about it— Banger was one spark plug short of an engine.

"Look," said Tooter. "Eight years ago, I would have been ten years older than Hooter was three years before I was half the age I am now."

"As for me," said Hooter. "Ten years ago I would have been three years older than Tooter was eight years before I was a third of my present age."

How old were Tooter and Hooter?

[Hint 41; Solution 43]

The Wizard's Sum

```
    4  5  2  6
+   2  7  5  8
─────────────
    7  2  8  4
-   3  4  1  5
─────────────
    3  8  6  9
+   3  8  2  6
─────────────
    7  6  9  5
```

ONE NIGHT as Little Lucy was tucked up in bed, she started to think about how difficult sums were at school. If only they were easy. Suddenly, a friendly wizard appeared holding a magic slate with a sum written on it.

"This slate is for you," said the wizard. "The sum you see written on it looks tricky, but watch closely and it will soon become easy." With that he vanished. So Lucy looked and looked but nothing changed. Then something strange happened. One digit disappeared from each of the seven rows and the gaps closed up to leave three columns of digits; then another vanished from each row to leave two columns; then another digit vanished so that there was one column. But each time a set of seven digits disappeared a valid sum remained.

When Lucy awoke the next morning the slate was gone. It must have all been a dream. Oh, well, time for school and some more difficult sums!

What were the three sets of disappearing digits?

[Hint 44; Solution 41]

Glasses and Lasses

"HEY DADDY," said Jill, "I'm feeling quite ill,"
    "Today, I'm not a well daughter,"
So he bent to her will and went up the hill,
To fetch five units of water.

On reaching the well, he suddenly fell,
And shattered his pail on the road,
But spying two lasses with cylindrical glasses,
He saw how to carry his load.

They're negligibly thick, he saw rather quick,
Praising himself for sagacity,
And what made it right was that both had same height,
Though obviously different capacity.

Sixteen and four were their volumes to pour,
And Dad filled the first up with water,
The second had none, but purely for fun,
He still took it back to his daughter.

"Just tell me," snarled Jill, going in for the kill,
"How we measure out five with these glasses?
Five from sixteen, that's a bit of a dream,"
Dad wished he'd eloped with the lasses.

How can sixteen units be reduced to five with these two cylindrical glasses?

[Hint 12; Solution 9]

68

Seeing Red

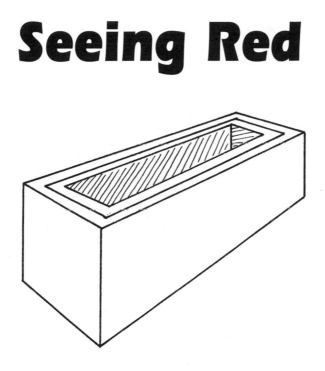

IN A SHOP storeroom stood a red box with a blue one inside, both having their only open end at the top. The fit was so exact that no space remained between the five pairs of box walls, and the tops of the two boxes were level.

Unfortunately, Mr. Tremble the manager had red phobia. In fact, his condition was so severe that he even had to wear black lipstick to look in the mirror. There was no alternative: the red box had to be dealt with, so he ordered Mr. Smart, his assistant, to paint the box a different color. However, Mr. Smart had no intention of spending time with a paint brush. He had discovered that the red box also fitted tightly inside the blue on all hidden walls; thus the color red could largely be concealed except for a small protrusion. The width of a box wall was 2mm.

How far did the red box protrude out of the blue?

[Hint 1; Solution 12]

Alf and Bert

S AID ALF to Bert "The last time we met, our ages were both prime
numbers, and when I was a quarter of the age I am now, you were
that age plus half the age your father would have been thirty years previous to when he was six times the age you would have been when I was
half your age."

Said Bert to Alf "I'm off to the pub."

How old were Alf and Bert the last time they met?

[Hint 18; Solution 17]

MATCHING
SWITCHES

I̲N A WOOD-CUTTING factory, four large sawing machines stand in a windowless room. Each machine has an on/off switch attached, there being no doubt as to which switch controls which machine. Outside the door to the room are four backup on/off switches, one for each machine inside. The power for each machine must first pass through the backup switch and then the attached switch before reaching the saw. The problem is, Arthur Fumble, the new manager, cannot decide how these backup switches match with the machines inside the room.

One day, Jimmy, the manager's brother visits. Arthur takes him inside the sawing room where all four machines are at work and explains the problem. Jimmy announces that he intends to leave the room and that when he returns he will be able to correctly match the four switches outside the room to the four machines inside. Jimmy works alone; he cannot see the machines from outside the room, but solves the problem purely by operating switches.

How is it possible?

[Hint 21; Solution 30]

Hail Clip

A LF AND BERT were sitting in the pub pondering over a ring-shaped cardboard beer mat (shown above).

Said Bert, "how can you move half of the letters to form the words HAIL CLIP reading clockwise?" With that, Alf produced a pair of scissors and with seven radial cuts, and a subsequent repositioning of letters, completed the task. "Very nice," said Bert, "but I could have done it with only one cut."

How is it possible?

[Hint 15; Solution 19]

The Giant's Castle

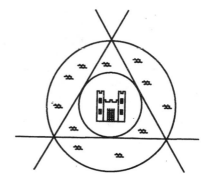

IN THE DARK AGES, in a remote part of Scotland, there once lived a fourteen-foot-tall giant called Scrambo, who used to terrorize the local villagers by chasing them with his stick. They were so scared of him that when he ordered them to build him a small castle to live in, they quietly agreed. Fortunately for the villagers, Scrambo was rather stupid, and chose flat land instead of the usual high ground.

An annular moat was dug around a central circular region, and the excavated soil was evenly distributed over the central region. There it was flattened to its original density to make a platform for the castle. The buckets of soil were raised from the moat with the aid of three wooden poles which spanned the moat. Each pole was three times the height of the giant, and each just touched the central region and intersected at the outer circumference of the moat.

Now the vertical distance from the bottom of the moat to the top of the platform was exactly equal to that part of a pole spanning the moat. When a pole was seated halfway across the flat moat bottom it just reached the top of the platform.

What was the width and depth of the excavated moat?

[Hint 36; Solution 48]

The Postman Puzzle

POSTMAN NAT delivered all ten of his letters in Ten-on-sea to four single-occupier cottages. Of the four numbers delivered, Tom and Nap received the only pair that differed by the number of letters that the postman had after completing his delivery round, no two cottages receiving the same number.

How many letters did Stan receive?

[Hint 19; Solution 4]

Leonardo's
Bathtime Puzzle

A s LEONARDO DA VINCI splashed around in his black bathtub contemplating how to make his new mechanical fire-breathing dragon expel flames, he turned his attention to an amusement he had recently been given by a merchant. It consisted of eight wooden blocks each with an engraved letter on it. The letters had to be arranged in their box according to the following rules:

(1) H was two places to the left of U;
(2) T was three places to the left of M;
(3) A was two places to the right of U;
(4) X was two places to the right of O.

However, the instructions stated that exactly one relationship was a lie. Of course, Leonardo soon realized there were many possible solutions. Then, just as he was recovering the soap from between his toes in the water he saw his arrangement, which made no particular word in the box, with the M four places from H and three to the right of the W.

What was Leonardo's solution?

[Hint 14; Solution 36]

CARTS OF COAL

Iᴺ Vɪᴄᴛᴏʀɪᴀɴ London, there was a coal yard at the top of a steep hill which customers would visit with their horse and cart. The yard sold two different size bags of coal, one being a two-digit number *ab* (*a* does not multiply *b* here) times the weight of the other. One day, Dirty Des turned up with his horse Neddy and asked for a number *c* of large bags and a number *d* of small bags to make the number *e* of hundredweight that his horse could pull. Shortly afterwards, Greasy Graham appeared with his horse Dobbin and asked for a number *f* of large bags and a number *g* of small bags to get the number *h* of hundredweight that Dobbin could pull.

Each of *a, b, c, d, e, f, g,* and *h* was a single digit, no two digits being equal and none of them being zero or one.

What were the weights of the large and small bags?

[Hint 4; Solution 13]

HINTS

1. *Seeing Red*
Let the base and open end of the red box both have dimensions XY and let the height be Z. Let the base and open end for the blue box be $X'Y'$ and the height Z', where X' fits into X, Y' fits Y, and Z' fits Z. We must then have $Z' = Z\text{-}2$, $X' = X\text{-}4$ and $Y' = Y\text{-}4$, taking into account the box walls.

2. *Paw Poem*
Each word contributes in some way to the answer.

3. *Doors to Freedom*
The prisoner must alternate exits and entrances. Let the unknown entrance be X. Then the possible orders are (a) -A-F-X, (b) -F-A-X, (c) X-A-F, (d) -X-F-A, (e) -A-X-F, or (f) -F-X-A, where a hyphen indicates an exit door.

4. *Carts of Coal*
The equations to be solved are as follows:

$$y = abx$$
$$cx + dy = e$$
$$fx + gy = h$$

where ab represents a two-digit number ($10a + b$), and x and y are the weights of the small and large bags of coal, respectively.

5. *The Wizard's Spell*
Count Lettuce means—and what are the two types of lettuce?!

6. *Duck to Cat*
If the cat pops his head up from the other side of the wall how is it possible to see it in the diagram?

7. *The Torn Message*
The word DO, meaning a party, must appear in the solution.

8. *Spot the Dice*
Since opposite faces of a die total 7, from A, the orientation of the three for the fifth die allows a 1 or 6 on top.

9. *Bye Bye Alibi*
Write down TIPS THE BRUSHED CHEFS, above each letter write down the letter that precedes it, and below each letter write the letter that comes next in the alphabet.

10. *The Two Jacks*
Let the ace be 1 and the jack be 11.

11. *Cubic Hexagon*
Do we have to always see three faces of a cube?

12. *Glasses and Lasses*
If we tilt the full larger glass until the water level reaches from the highest point on the base to the lowest point of the open top (i.e. the side view is the diagonal of a rotated rectangle), half of the water will spill out leaving 8 units. How can the smaller glass be used to reduce the amount to 3 units?

13. *Cups and Balls*
If only one statement is true, that statement must be the only one to have the correct number.

14. *Leonardo's Bathtime Puzzle*
Investigation should show that the last two relationships are inconsistent with the rules no matter which one is discarded. Consider why the bathtub is black, what the letters AHMOTUWX have in common, why the character Leonardo is significant and what ". . . from between his toes in the water he saw his . . ." means.

15. *Hail Clip*
The single cut does not have to be a straight line. How could all letters be affected so that half of them move?

16. *Deleting Sheep*
Total each row and column and see how much above 30 each one is. Two numbers totaling the excess must disappear from each row and column. There might be several possible pairs for each row and column so focus on one row or column and deduce the consequences for each possible pair.

17. Cons and Conjurors

The 1 can only be with the 2 or 4. If it is with 2, then we must have 5-3 and 4-6, and 9 cannot appear.

18. Alf and Bert

If A and B are Alf and Bert's present ages, and a and b their ages when Alf was half Bert's age, then the equation that arises is as follows:

$$B - 3A/4 = (A/4) + (6b - 30)/2$$

19. The Postman Puzzle

There are five ways that we can divided 10 into four numbers so that no two numbers are the same. These are 0,1,2,7; 0,1,3,6; 0,1,4,5; 0,2,3,5 and 1,2,3,4. However, Postman Nat has no letters left to deliver and there is no number pair with zero difference. Some special assumption is needed about one of the cottage tenants!

20. Breaking the Circuit

If just one interchange restores the original arrangement, then there are exactly two rows and two columns of batteries each totaling 10 volts.

21. Matching Switches

The brother labels all the switches and before leaving the room switches two off and leaves two on. Outside the room, how is it possible to identify which two switches correspond to the two "on" switches in the room?

22. The Six Digits

Try using powers.

23. Packing Boxes

Let the depth of a chocolate box be D, the width be W, and the length be L. Comparing the top side of the rectangular view with the bottom side we have
$$3D + 2L = 2W + L$$
so that
$$3D + L = 2W$$

24. Synchronizing Watches

Each time the minute hand rotates 360 degrees, the hour hand rotates 30 degrees.

25. Cannibals
It takes five cannibals 2/5 hours to eat the first victim.

26. The Stolen Sweets
Let the number for Mollusc be x and that for Tweaker be y. The number taken by Tweaker is $y/3$, leaving Mollusc with $x-y/3$.

27. The Missing Rum
Write out the six ways that A and D can be two apart. Since B is on the right of C or E, eliminate the possibilities that do not have two adjacent spaces.

28. Complex Crossword 1
Across: Remove the letters "hole" from "denial to Enoch" to give a reverse-sequence word meaning "restrained."
Down: The letters "royal pen" minus the letters "on" give an anagram for a word meaning "actor."
Across: Add the letters "rain" to "bitter day" and subtract the letters "dry tea" to get "islands."
Down: The letter "l" from "lucidity" is crossed out of "revile crepes" to give a reversed-letter word meaning "sense."
Across: "Sell pie" is a pure anagram of a "figure."
Down: A "writer" appears in sequence in ". . . one's bitter."
Across: "Tea" means "t" and is added to the letters "divine" to make an anagram for "tempted."
Down: The word "first" indicates first letters of words.
Across: A word meaning collar has in-sequence letters in "Bella pelting us."
Down: Take the letters "rex" and "p" from "expire" and add "d" for an anagram.

29. Tiny Tum's Homework
What arithmetic sign could raise the 15 towards the 208?

30. Mumble Meadow
The two-hour relation cannot start at 9 A.M. because one hour later neither red nor green pajamas were worn, and because neither blue nor yellow is permitted at 10 A.M., no color is possible.

31. Truth and Treasure
How many coins must the guard be protecting for each statement assumed true?

32. Colored Kits
Consider all the positions that the relations "The pink was with . . ." and "The red was . . ." can be in and check these with the condition that only one item in each column is correctly positioned.

33. Fair Game
The lion still has two legs and a tail when it's dead but not as seen in the diagram.

34. Fantasy Island
Two eliminations can be made straight away, giving Paradise Palace second and Good Elf third. Where can the given relations be positioned without contradictions?

35. Complex Crossword 2
Across: A word meaning "bed" is written backwards in "field archaeology."

Down: Remove the letters "today" from "do try paint" to get an anagram of a word meaning "mark."

Across: Take the letters "bear laugh" from "are nought laborious" to give a word meaning "well known," with letters in sequence.

Down: The letters "deer chin" give an anagram for a word meaning wealthier.

Across: A word meaning "to decay" is contained in "whisper Isherwood" in sequence.

Down: Remove the letters "all use" from "usual detail" to give an anagram for a word meaning "to scrutinize."

Across: "Primarily" tells you to look at initial letters of words only to get a word meaning "chief."

Down: Take the letters "heal" from "a neon lighter" to get an anagram of a gas.

Across: The clue word is "finish," and the synonym is contained in the words "wooden door" in sequence.

Down: Take the letters "Reg said be in" and remove the letters "a grin" to leave an anagram for "nearby."

36. The Giant's Castle
Drop a perpendicular (line at right-angles) from one of the poles to the circle center, from the point where the pole touches the inner circle. Complete a right-angled triangle by joining the circle center to a triangle corner formed by the same pole. Express the width of the moat and the pole span in terms of the inner-circle radius.

37. *Round the Table*
The initial seating arrangement (clockwise or counterclockwise) is Throgmorton, Horace, Gertrude, Arbuthnot, Prigwick, and Delilah.

38. *Square Words*
Both the bottom left and top right corners have an M.

39. *Complex Crossword 3*
Across: A reversed-letter word is contained in "more temporary business" with the letters "pry" removed.
Down: "licc trap" is an anagram.
Across: Look at the initial letters of words.
Down: "scary doom" contains a reversed-letters word.
Across: Take "coy star has" and remove the letters "oars" for an anagram.
Down: Remove the letter "n" from "modern object" to give a reversed-letter word.
Across: Remove the letter "j" from "fur object" to give an in-sequence word.
Down: "Forefront of" indicates initial letters.
Across: Take "General Reilly" and remove the letters "real energy."
Down: Remove the letters "comment lone sir" from "morose internment cell."

40. *Untying the Knot*
Due to his relationship in time to Irma and also the possible groom first names at 1 P.M., Danny can only be married at 11 A.M. or 12 noon.

41. *Old Automobiles*
Remember to take half of Tooter's present age plus 3 from Hooter's present age. What is taken from Tooter's age?

42. *Library Logic*
Write down the four ways that D--G can fit into the seven available places.

43. *Complex Crossword 4*
Across: A word meaning "widow" appears in sequence in "robber eavesdropping."
Down: "Ice bread" with "e" removed is an anagram of a compound.
Across: A word meaning "animate" is found in the anagram "ripe sin."

Down: Add "r" to "gross Arab meals" to get a reverse-sequence word meaning "show up."

Across: Remove "r" from "real" to get an anagram of a drink.

Down: Reverse the letters of "our," and add them to "pavement" to get a reverse-sequence word for "steam."

Across: The letters "takes whore" have "awe" and "h" removed.

Down: A word meaning "succession" comes from "see rise" with no "e."

Across: Remove the letters "a" and "s" from "reads" to get a word meaning "Communist."

Down: A "sense organ" is contained in "heard" in sequence.

44. The Wizard's Sum

The seven-line sum can be broken down into three three-line addition sums involving lines 1–3, 3–5, and 5–7.

45. Parking Space

The relation (1) beginning "The spaceship from Delta . . ." can only be first or third, because if it were in second place no spaceship would fit, and in fourth place no planet would fit. What about the possible positions of the relation (2) beginning "Wop was from neither Blip nor Vulcan . . . ?"

46. The Logic Cards

Labeling the statements A, B, and C from left to right, first consider the consequences of the combinations where C is true then false in the middle. Then consider these two possibilities when C is at one end. Do the same with B.

SOLUTIONS

1. Cons and Conjurors
The pairings were as follows: 2-3, 4-1, 5-8, 7-6, 10-12, and 11-9. Number 1 can only be with the 2 or 4. If it is with 2, then we must have 5-3 and 4-6, and 9 cannot appear. If the 1 is with 4 then we either have 2-3 or 5-3. With the latter we have 7-6, and no 8 is possible. With the former we have 7-6, 10-12, 11-9, and 5-8, and the solution follows.

2. Doors to Freedom
The order is CFDABE. The guards entered through doors A and F and exited at door B. The prisoner must alternate exits and entrances. Let the unknown entrance be X. Then the possible orders are (a) -A-F-X, (b) -F-A-X, (c) -X-A-F, (d) -X-F-A, (e) -A-X-F, or (f) -F-X-A, where a hyphen indicates an exit door.

Neither (a) nor (c) are possible, since A is followed by B or E and neither leads to F. Since A can only be preceded by D, (e) and (f) are possible as DA-X-F and -F-XDA, respectively. With D used, door F can now only be preceded by C, so we have DA-XCF and CF-XDA. Door B must occupy the remaining hyphen (third door is an exit) so X=E but C cannot follow E for the former; and for the latter, B cannot follow F. Considering what follows F and precedes A, (b) is possible only as -FDA-X and (d) as -X-FDA. For (d), door B (exit) must occupy a hyphen, but cannot be followed by F, and if it is first, neither the C nor E that must follow lead to the remaining letter E or C, respectively. Finally, with (b), only C remains to precede F, B must occupy the final hyphen (exit) with X=E.

3. The Torn Message
The message was GOUT ISLE NUNS A DO (here DO means party).

4. The Postman Puzzle
Stan received 2 letters because the postman lived in one of the cottages!

First, the red herring! The name Postman Nat has 10 alphabetic letters and the names Tom, Stan and Nap exhaust these. However, we cannot have two cottages with the same number of letters so this idea won't work. There are five ways that we can divide 10 into four numbers so that no two numbers are the same. These are 0,1,2,7; 0,1,3,6; 0,1,4,5; 0,2,3,5; and 1,2,3,4. However, Postman Nat has no letters left to deliver, and there is no number pair with zero difference. So let us assume that Postman Nat lives in one of the cottages so that he delivers a number of letters to himself. He can then have some letters after completing his delivery. There must be only one pair of the four numbers with this number as their difference and neither of the pair is this difference (Nat is neither Tom nor Nap). Only if Nat has 3 in 1,2,3,4 can we satisfy this condition, with Tom and Nap having 1 and 4 letters (order unimportant) and Stan (who is not Nat) having 2. Notice that the consonants in "Ten-on-sea" (tenancy) are the initials of the four occupants (including Nat) and that the phrase "delivered his letters in tenancy" indicates Nat's occupancy of a cottage.

5. Spot the Dice
The missing top numbers are B=5, E=1, F=3, the missing front numbers are B=4, C=2, and D=1. Since opposite faces of a die total 7, from A, the orientation of the three at E allows a 1 or 6 on top. Since 6 already appears it must be 1. At F, the top must be 1, 3, 4, or 6, and only 3 is unused. So 5 is on top at B. From A, the orientation of the 3 must give 2 or 5 at C, and only 2 is available. At D, 1, 2, 5, or 6 is possible, but only 1 is unused. This leaves 4 at the front at B.

6. Bye Bye Alibi
The entry in Nora's diary can be decoded as SHOT SID ASTRIDE BIDET.

7. The Two Jacks
Let the ace be 1 and the jack be 11. If the cards are set out in the order ten, ace, three, jack (10, 1, 3, 11) and each number is replaced by the letter in that alphabetic position, we get the word JACK. So one jack arises from the interpreted card order and the other must be far right.

8. Autumn Acres
The eggs are at the CASTLE. One letter comes from each animal as follows.

Blackie the crow
Sycamore. A table can be made for the two cases for each tree when it either is or is not that tree.

tree	is not	is
oak	o	s *or* f
willow	w	o *or* s
sycamore	s	w *or* f
fir	f	s *or* o

We now need to select three rows from the four so that the "is not" tree from the missing row appears in all the "is" items for the chosen three rows.

Burrows the mole

Elm. Remove the letters "saying nothing" from "his tangy lemon" to leave an anagram of the solution.

Timid the squirrel

Larch. Let us make a table of the possible positions—

	pine	larch	ash	birch
1	*	*	*	
2	*	*	*	
3			*	*
4	*			*

—where the * denotes a possible position. The pine and the ash must be next to each other. There are four ways this can occur. Only with the pine at 2 and the ash at 3 do we get a solution.

Spike the hedgehog

Cedar. The possibilities for the willow and ash are w-a--, -w-a-, --w-a, a-w--, -a-w-, and --a-w. In these, the oak and pine must be adjacent, and the cedar must be to the right of the oak. This gives the possibilities opwca, powca, opacw, and poacw with the cedar second from the right in all cases.

Hoppity the rabbit

The letter "T" can replace the word tea (see Tutorial).

Squeaker the mouse

Ash. The solutions are:

time	friend	location	tree
8	Meryl	barn	elm
9	Weeny	viaduct	ash
10	Tipsey	pond	oak

9. Glasses and Lasses

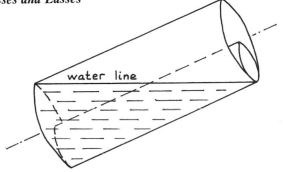

water line

If we tilt the larger glass full of water until the water level reaches from the highest point on the base to the lowest point of the open top, the larger glass will be half full and will contain eight units. Since the larger jug has sixteen units volume and the smaller has four, then their equal height h guarantees that the larger radius r is twice the smaller. This arises from the formula for the volume of a cylinder V,

$$V = \pi r^2 h$$

where π is about 3.14. If we now lay the smaller glass inside the larger, up against the lower side of the larger (as shown), the axis up through the center of the larger glass will lie along one side of the smaller glass. This means that three-quarters of the smaller glass (three units) will lie below the water level and a quarter (1 unit) will be above. This introduction of the smaller glass allows three units of water to spill out, leaving five units in the larger glass.

10. Cups and Balls
There were three balls under each, and the third statement was true. If only one statement is true, that statement must be the only one to have the correct number. The numbers one, two, and four appear in more than one statement. The number three appears in only the third statement, so that must be the true one.

11. Paw Poem
It does not refer to anything. Taking the first letter of each word, we discover it's complete and utter nonsense.

12. Seeing Red

The red box protruded 20mm out of the top of the blue one. Let the base and open end of the red box both have dimensions XY, and let the height be Z. Let the base and open end for the blue box be $X'Y'$ and the height Z', where X' fits into X, Y' fits Y, and Z' fits Z. We must then have $Z' = Z-2$, $X' = X-4$, and $Y' = Y-4$, taking into account the box walls. If $X = Y$, then when the red is fitted into the blue, we cannot find two of X,Y,Z which will fit into two of X', Y',Z'. So let $X > Y(X' > Y')$—N.B. > means greater than. This means that X will not fit X',Y'; Y will not fit Y'; Z will not fit Z'. So X must fit in Z' with some protrusion, and since Y will not fit in Y' it can only fit in X' with Z in Y'. Thus

$$X > X' > Y > Y' > Z > Z'$$

with $X' = Y + 4$, $Y' = Z + 4$. We then have $X = Z' + 18$, which relates the new red box vertical dimension X, to that of the blue Z'. Adding the base width of 2mm gives the solution.

13. Carts of Coal

The large bag was 16/21 hundredweight and the small bag was 1/42 hundredweight. The problem is to find the different digits $a,b,c,...,h$ in the eight-digit set 2,3,4,...,9 which allow a solution to the equations

$$y = abx$$
$$cx + dy = e$$
$$fx + gy = h$$

where ab represents a two-digit number ($10a + b$), and x and y are the weights of the small and large bags of coal, respectively. The only solution occurs for

$$y = 32x$$
$$8x + 5y = 4$$
$$6x + 9y = 7$$

so that the solution for x and y follows.

14. *Complex Crossword 1*

			N						
	A	X	E		L	A	P	E	L
P			S		U		L		
E			B	R	I	T	A	I	N
R			I		N		Y		
C	O	N	T	A	I	N	E	D	
E							R		
I	N	V	I	T	E	D			
V						I			
E	L	L	I	P	S	E			

Across: contained
Across: Britain
Across: ellipse
Across: invited
Across: lapel

Down: player
Down: perceive
Down: Nesbit
Down: Luini
Down: die

15. *The Wizard's Spell*

The sorcerer changed the count into A RAT. All the consonants that appear should do so three times each and all the vowels six times each. Thus these four letters are missing. Note that Count Lettuce (count letters) indicates how to proceed with the problem!

16. *Duck to Cat*

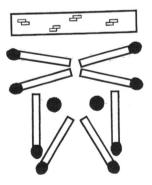

The view is of the cat's reflection in the water as it pops up from behind the wall!

17. *Alf and Bert*

Alf and Bert were two and five years old, respectively, the last time they met. If A and B are Alf and Bert's present ages, and a and b are their ages when Alf was half Bert's age, then

$$B—3A/4 = (A/4) + (6b—30)/2$$

Since their ages have always had the same difference, we have

$$B—A = 3b—15 = b—a$$

and since $2a = b$, then $a = 3$, $b = 6$. So their ages differ by 3. Since all primes (except 2) are odd and differ by an even number we can only have 2 and 5, Bert being the older of the two. The father plays no part in the problem!

18. *Cannibals*

It took four hours and thirty-four minutes for one cannibal to be left.

It took five cannibals 2/5 hours to eat the first victim, four cannibals 2/4 hours for the second, three cannibals 2/3 hours for the third, two cannibals 2/2 hours for the fourth and one cannibal 2/1 hours for the fifth.

One could argue that stomach contents increase a cannibal's edible volume when he is the victim. However, if the further interpretation is granted that these contents also turn a cannibal as consumer into more than one cannibal, the original solution is restored!

19. *Hail Clip*

First, Alf's method with seven cuts. Interchange the I next to the C with the L next to the P, and interchange the A and P. Bert's method uses a single cut along the circle running through the middle of the letters. If the outer ring formed is now rotated one place counterclockwise, half the letters will be moved to form HAIL CLIP!

20. *The Stolen Sweets*

Mollusc has 20 sweets and Tweaker has 15 sweets. Let Mollusc have x sweets and Tweaker y sweets. The number taken by Tweaker is $y/3$, which leaves Mollusc with $x-y/3$. Mollusc retrieves the same number, which is $(x-y/3)/3$, so we have

$$y = 35-x$$
and also
$$y/3 = (x-y/3)/3$$
$$4y = 3x$$

and the solution follows.

Another way is to reason that if the number of sweets being transferred, q say, is equal to a third of Tweaker's original amount, r say, or Mollusc's remainder, s say, then these two amounts must be equal, $r = s$. Since q is one third of r and the total consists of the sum of three numbers—the sweets transferred q, Tweaker's original amount $3q$, and Mollusc's remainder $3q$—then we have a total of $7q = 35$, so $q=5$ and the result follows.

21. *The Missing Rum*

Dirty Dog drank the rum. The order is Awful Andrew, Cruel Colin, Dirty Dog, Evil Eddie and Big Bob. Since Dirty Dog is two places from Awful Andrew, the two adjacent places that Big Bob, and either Cruel Colin or Evil Eddie occupy must be at the end of the row. This leaves D-A--, A-D--, --D-A, or --A-D. Big Bob, being to the right of his adjacent partner, must occupy the last or second position. This leaves D-A-B, A-D-B, -BD-A, or -BA-D. Only the second case allows three consecutive places in alphabetical order as ACDEB.

22. *Breaking the Circuit*

The batteries are $A=D=2$, $B=3$, and $C=4$. The juxtaposed batteries should be B in row 1, column 3, and D in row 3, column 1. If just one interchange restores the original arrangement, then there are exactly two rows and two columns of batteries, each totaling 10 volts. The remaining two rows and two columns are involved in the interchange. We now take the six combinations where two rows are both 10 volts and set them equal. For example, for rows 2 and 4, we have $A+C+2D=2A+C+D$ so that $A=D$, and use the fact that the total of all batteries is 40 volts, i.e. $5(A+D)+2(2B+C)=40$. By experimenting with possible values, we find five solutions: $A=D=1$, $B=4$, $C=7$; $A=D=2$, $C=3$, $D=4$; $A=D=3$, $B=2$, $C=1$; $A=B=2$, $C=1$, $D=4$; or $A=B=3$, $C=4$,

$D=1$—only the first three allowing a single juxtaposition. The condition that exactly three batteries total 10 volts reduces us to the second case (4+3+3).

23. Complex Crossword 2

		A	X	E		N		
	P		U			I		
C	R	A	D	L	E		T		B
	I		I		N		R		E
	N	O	T	O	R	I	O	U	S
	T				I		G		I
					C		E	N	D
P	E	R	I	S	H		N		E
					E				
		C	A	R	D	I	N	A	L

Across: cradle
Across: notorious
Across: perish
Across: cardinal
Across: end

Down: print
Down: enriched
Down: audit
Down: nitrogen
Down: beside

24. *The Codfish Kung Fuer*

The Codfish kung fuer was Dibdib, who sat to Walter the Wailer's left.

Wipsey	Babble	Polyp	Herman
Squiggle	Flapper	Dibdib	Walter
Stutter	Flicker	Worm	Crabtree
Hogweed	Moron	Pits	Stinker

The relations that have to be fitted together are

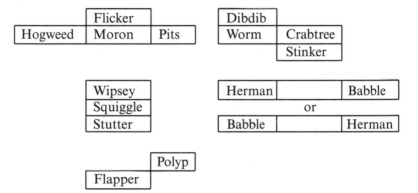

There is only one way this is possible.

25. *Deleting Sheep*

3	8		7	5	3	4	
7		4	3	9	5		2
5	3	9		1	4	8	
	5	2	5	4		5	9
1	3	5	8		7		6
8		1	6	9		5	1
	7	9		2	3	5	4
6	4		1		8	3	8

26. *Synchronizing Watches*

The time on Sally's watch is 10:05:27 A.M. Each time the minute hand rotates 360 degrees, the hour hand rotates 30 degrees. If x is the number of rotations of the minute hand between consecutive alignments, then

$$360x-360 = 30x$$

where the subtracted 360 occurs because x is greater than one. This gives the hands in alignment every 12/11 rotations of the minute hand, there being 11 alignments every 12 hours. Sally keeps subtracting 1/11 hour off her time at each chime believing it occurs on the hour. There are 21 adjustments before Sally sees the clock again (at the 22nd alignment) so 21/11 hours subtracted from 24 hours gives the above solution (1/11 hour is 5 minutes, 27 seconds, to the nearest second).

27. *Tiny Tum's Homework*

The missing number is 13. The two signs that are missing are "minus" on the left-hand side and "multiply" on the right-hand side:

$$208 - 13 = 15 \times 13$$

I published the first problem of the form $xz ? xy = zx ! xy$ in *The Daily Telegraph (UK)* on 30 October 1993. The only solutions are

$$27 - 24 = 72 / 24$$
$$49 - 47 = 94 / 47$$

28. *Complex Crossword 3*

						R	O	B	E
				A	X	E		O	
			P			L		R	
		B	A	R	O	M	E	T	E	R
			R			N		D	
			T		M	T		O	
			I		O			M	
			C	L	O	U	D	S	
I	L	L		D				A	
		E		Y	A	C	H	T	S

Across: barometer Down: particle
Across: clouds Down: moody
Across: yachts Down: boredom
Across: robe Down: at
Across: ill Down: relent

29. *Square Words*

```
F I R M
I D E A
R E N T
M A T E
```

30. *Matching Switches*

Let us label the switches inside the room A, B, C, D, and the ones outside the room a, b, c, d. If all four machines are running, all eight switches must be switched on initially. Before the brother leaves the room, he switches A and B off, leaving C and D on. Of course, only machines C and D are now running.

Outside the room, he tests all six combinations of exactly two switches turned off until he hears no noise. Only one of the six combinations can achieve this. For example, if turning only a and b off produces silence then he knows that a/b corresponds to C/D (both on), and so c/d corresponds to A/B, though he still cannot decide the precise matching within the pair (e.g., whether switch b matches C or D). Outside the room, he now switches one of the two "on" switches off and one of the two "off" switches on; so, following our example, he could set a on, b off, c on, and d off. When he returns to the room, only one of C or D machines will now be on, say D. This machine matches switch c (on) and so C matches switch d. He then tests A and B switches to see which turns one of the machines on. Let's say it's A. This machine matches switch a (on), and so B must match b.

31. *The Six Digits*

The three solutions involve the use of powers $4^3 + 1^2 = 65$, $4^1 + 2^5 = 36$, $35 + 1^4 = 6^2$. This puzzle was inspired by a classic puzzle which involves the digits 2, 3, 4, and a + and = sign. Each of the six characters must be used once and once only to make an equation. The solution is $4 + 5 = 3^2$.

32. *Seven Secrets*

Scroll. The scroll indicates that sometimes one secret unlocks the next. Also, taking the first letter from each of the first six solutions gives something to get past the dragon in the seventh secret.

First Secret. Taking the first letter from each dwarf, we must have the order AE or EA; with R-H--, -R-H-, or --R-H; and E--T or -E--T. The only possibility that fits is EARTH.

Second Secret. Of bricks, soil, water, bellows, and cloak, only SOIL corresponds with the solution to the first task.

Third Secret. An insect, a heroic day, dried grass, and an expanse of water must be put in the order (a), (b), (c), and (d). The first is BEE, the second D(-DAY), the third HAY, and the fourth SEA. These sound like the letters in the order. So (a) HAY (dried grass), (b) BEE (an insect), (c) SEA (an expanse of water), (d) D-DAY (a heroic day). The first choice is DRIED GRASS.

Fourth Secret. A goose, warrior, horse, or crocodile must be bribed. The first choice from the previous task (hay) is used to bribe the HORSE.

Fifth Secret. The names are anagrams of dangerous, lantern, vicious, and spiteful. Manichop had to look at the sixth task to discover that only the gazelle from the fifth task could provide one of the four choices on the tunnel plaque (Illumination). He had to unravel Nentarl to get LANTERN to cross the ravine.

Sixth Secret. Of map, illumination, headgear, and knife, only ILLU-MINATION corresponded to one of the choices in the fifth task.

Seventh Secret. Following the scroll, the first letters from the first six secrets are ESDHLI which is an anagram of SIIIELD. This allows Manichop to get past the dragon.

Thus the seven secrets are EARTH, SOIL, DRIED GRASS, HORSE, LANTERN, ILLUMINATION, SHIELD. The rearranged first letters give SHIELD.

33. *Cubic Hexagon*

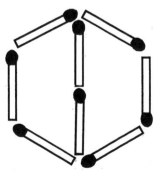

With the added line, one is looking close up at one edge of a cube whose two visible faces are receding.

34. Packing Boxes

The smallest number of boxes is 255. Let the depth of a chocolate box be D, the width be W, and the length be L. Comparing the top side of the rectangular view with the bottom side, we have

$$3D + 2L = 2W + L$$

so that

$$3D + L = 2W \ (1)$$

Comparing the left edge with the right edge, we also have

$$2L + D = 3W \ (2)$$

Multiplying (1) by 2 and subtracting (2), we have

$$W = 5D$$

that is, 5 depths equals 1 width. Putting W into (1) gives

$$L = 7D$$

that is, 7 depths equals 1 length. This means that there must be 5 lengths to 7 widths as we go down into the packing case, so we must have 35 depths. Keeping the same box pattern all the way down—which (looking downwards) consists of 5 widths, 2 lengths, and 6 depths—our calculation is 5x7 + 2x5 + 6x35 = 255.

35. Fantasy Island

1	Happy Herman	Doris the Mermaid	Dungblock Dungeon
2	Wally the Wizard	Matilda the Witch	Paradise Palace
3	Good Elf	Wicked Queen	Cobblers Castle
4	Pixie Nose	Sugar Plum Fairy	Vegetable Patch

By elimination, Paradise Palace must be second and the Good Elf third, with Happy Herman first and Pixie Nose fourth. The Vegetable Patch is the only possible correct house name, so Dungblock Dungeon is first.

Since the Vegetable Patch is fourth, the Cobblers-Castle-or-Dungblock-Dungeon relation cannot be fourth; it can only be first—and that, therefore, is where Doris the Mermaid or Matilda the Witch is. Then only Matilda the Witch can be correct in second place—leaving Doris the Mermaid first, the Sugar Plum Fairy fourth, and the Wicked Queen third.

36. Leonardo's Bathtime Puzzle

WAXMOUTH. There are several allusions to a reflection in the puzzle. Leonardo da Vinci was well known for his mirror writing, a BLACK bathtub gives the best background for a reflection in water, all the letters AHMOTUWX remain the same after a left-right reflection, and the seemingly innocent line ". . . from between his toes *in the water he saw his . . . ,*" which needs to be read the right way.

So the three from four rules must apply *in the box*. Of course, the last two relationships (M-H, M-W) are inconsistent with these no matter which rule is a lie. However, when he sees his arrangement as reflected *in the water* these last two rules (unreflected since they're applied to what he sees in the water) are consistent with *just one* reflected arrangement with rule (3) being the lie. And they apply to WAXMOUTH in the water (HTUOMXAW in the box)—an idea he gets for how to make his fire-breathing dragon work!!!

37. *The Logic Cards*
If the cards are labeled A, B, and C from left to right, the correct order is CAB, with the first card false and the last two cards true. Suppose C is at the end of the line. Then if it is true (C_t) then it is false. If it is false (C_f) then the other end is true, thus $C_{f-?-t}$ or $-_{t-?-}C_f$, which shows that C can be at either end. Suppose C is in the middle. Then C_t gives the other two as false $-_fC_{t-f}$. If C_f, then at least one of the ends is true: $-_tC_{f-f}$, $-_fC_{f-t}$, $-_tC_{f-t}$. Suppose B_t. If it is in the middle, then all are true, which incorrectly gives C_t at the end of the line. If it is at one end, the middle one is true, which cannot be C because both ends are then false (see above)—so we can only have $B_tA_tC_f$ or $C_fA_tB_t$. Suppose B_f. If it is central, then at least one of the ends is false: $C_fB_fA_t$ or $A_tB_fC_f$ (using the above analysis for C_f). If it is at one end, the middle one is false: $A_tC_fB_f$ or $B_fC_fA_t$ (again using the C_f analysis). Six possibilities arise, and since A_t is in all of them, then the second and third places are true. The only solution is $C_fA_tB_t$.

38. *Mumble Meadow*

9 A.M.	Bertha	hippopotamus	blue
10 A.M.	Agatha	slug	green
11 A.M.	Cecil	centipede	red
12 noon	Herbert	wildebeest	yellow

The two-hour relation cannot start at 9 A.M., because one hour later neither red nor green pajamas were worn; and because neither blue nor yellow is permitted at 10 A.M., no color is possible. Since either Agatha or Herbert is at 10 A.M., the two-hour relation cannot begin at 10 A.M. either. So either Cecil or Bertha is at 11 A.M., as neither the slug nor wildebeest and without green pajamas; also neither red nor green pajamas are at 12 noon.

In the pajamas column, only blue can be correct at 9 A.M. So green is at 10 A.M., red at 11 A.M., and yellow at 12 noon. At 11 a.m., by elimination, only the centipede is possible, because the hippopotamus is at 9 A.M. (and only one can be correctly positioned), the wildebeest must be at 12 noon, and the slug at 10 A.M. In the name column, both Bertha and Agatha must be wrong. So either Cecil or Herbert is correct. If Cecil is correct, Herbert can only be at 10 A.M., and Agatha has nowhere to go. So Herbert is correct, Cecil must be at 11 A.M., Bertha at 9 A.M. and Agatha at 10 A.M.

39. The Torque Wrench

The five letters are R,O,B,E,K—making the word BROKE.

Weeder's Clue. 2(x-6)=3(x-10) giving x=18, which represents R.

Juggler's Clue. A table can be formed for the case of truthteller and liar for each fruit's statement.

	T	L
A	P/B	A/O
B	O/A	B/P
O	A/B	O/P
P	B/P	A/O

Only the orange appears in exactly one true statement, so the letter is O.

Little Side Clue. The letter B goes at the front of each of these five words to make before, benign, belittle, beside, bespoke. So this is the letter required.

Catering Clue. Clean the pans (9,3) is an anagram of elephants can. So E is the letter Fred wants.

Postman Clue. The Fiona/Ian (FI) and Harry/Lorna (HL) clues give the possibilities (with FI meaning F or I) FI,H,-,IF,L,-,-,- or FI,L, -,IF,H,-,-,- or FI,-,H,IF,-,L,-,- or FI,-,L,IF,-,H,-,- or FI,-,-,IF,H,-,-,L or FI,-,-,IF,L,-,-,H. The June and George clue eliminates the third and fourth possibilities. One of them must also occupy the second or third position, so that the Mark and Karen clue means that Karen must be in one of the last three places. In the first and second possibilities, K is eighth; in the fifth and sixth K is sixth or seventh. But K is next to neither L nor H, so the seventh and eighth are eliminated. Hence, K is the last letter.

40. Complex Crossword 4

					A	X	E		
E		C				A	S		
M		A				R	E	D	
B	E	R	E	A	V	E		R	
A		B			A		I		
R		I	N	S	P	I	R	E	
R		D			O		S		
A	L	E			U				
S			S	T	R	O	K	E	
S									

Across: bereave   Down: carbide
Across: inspire   Down: embarrass
Across: ale   Down: vapour
Across: stroke   Down: series
Across: red   Down: ear

41. The Wizard's Sum
Reading downwards, the digits in order of deletion are 4, 7, 2, 3, 8, 8, 7; 2, 5, 7, 1, 6, 3, 9; 5, 8, 4, 4, 9, 6, 6.

42. Round the Table
Reading either clockwise (C) or counterclockwise (A), we have Prigwick, Gertrude, Delilah, Horace, Arbuthnot, and Throgmorton. The starting positions (C or A) are Throgmorton, Horace, Gertrude, Arbuthnot, Prigwick, and Delilah. There are now only three arrangements where no person sits next to either of his two neighbors. These are Prigwick, Horace, Delilah, Arbuthnot, Throgmorton, Gertrude; Prigwick, Throgmorton, Gertrude, Delilah, Arbuthnot, Horace (which both have Prigwick next to Horace); and the given solution (which does not).

43. Old Automobiles
Tooter is twenty and Hooter is fifteen. Let Tooter's age be x and Hooter's age be y. Then

$$x—8 = 10 + y—(x/2 + 3)$$
$$y—10 = 3 + x—(2y/3 + 8)$$

We note that when y was one third of his present age we are talking about y—$y/3$ years ago. These equations reduce to

$$3x—2y = 30 \ (1)$$
$$5y—3x = 15 \ (2)$$

Adding (1) and (2) gives

$$3y = 45$$
$$y = 15 \ (3)$$

Placing (3) in (1) produces

$$3x = 60$$
$$x = 20 \ (4)$$

44. Fair Game

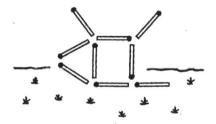

45. Truth and Treasure

There were 3,000 gold, 4,000 silver, and 5,000 bronze. Assume each statement to be true in turn and examine the consequences. If Dimwit is truthful, there are 3,000 silver, 5,000 bronze, and hence 4,000 gold. However, this would make Beefbrain truthful also. By symmetry, if Beefbrain is truthful, then so is Dimwit. Only with Thickplank truthful do we get the other statements false.

46. Colored Kits

1. yellow   brown   orange
2. purple   green   red
3. pink   blue   violet

Since a purple or yellow is first, the pink cannot be first so relation (1) "The pink was with . . ." must be second or third. Since this relation refers to a violet or orange in the third column, the relation (2) "The red was . . ." cannot be in the same place.

Suppose (2) is first and (1) is third. Then we have pink third, purple first, and yellow second, with all three correctly placed. However, only one should be in the correct position. Suppose (2) is third and (1) is second. Then pink is second, purple third, and yellow is first, none being correctly positioned. Suppose (2) is first and (1) second. In the Shorts column we then have brown second, green first, and blue third, with none correctly placed.

Suppose (2) is second and (1) is third. Then in the Shirts column we have pink third, purple second, and yellow first, with exactly one correctly placed. In the Shorts column, neither blue nor green can be correct; so brown is first, green second, and blue third. For the Socks column, red must be second, so both red and orange are incorrect, and violet is third with orange first.

47. *The Missing Sandwiches*
Their order is PaniC, O'HarA, NiB, RossI, OgdeN, ScroogE, and BuckeT. The last one of each spells CABINET, which is where the sanswiches are. The statements by O'Hara, Nib, and Ogden give the possibilities T-NAB, T-NBA, ABN-T, AB-N-T, BAN-T, and T-N-BA. Panic's statement gives C—I. The only combination of these where ScroogE is to the right of RossI is CABINET.

48. *The Giant's Castle*

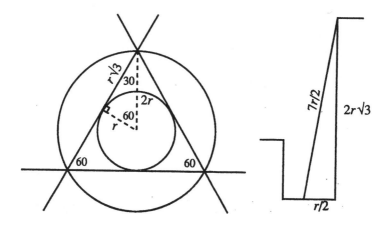

The moat was 12 feet wide and 10.39 feet deep. The 60-degree angle between a perpendicular from one of the poles to the center and a line from the center to a triangle corner forms part of a right-angled triangle. The first side is the inner circle radius r and the second side is $2r$. This gives the third side as $\sqrt{3}r$ and the length of the pole spanning the moat as $2\sqrt{3}r$, with the width of the moat as r. The triangle formed in the moat, with the pole span $2\sqrt{3}r$ as the height and $r/2$ as the base, has the hypotenuse $7r/2$, which is the full length of the pole equal to $3\times14=42$ feet. This gives the moat width r as 12 feet. Now the area of the inner circular region is $\sqrt{}r^2$ and that of the outer circle is $4\sqrt{}r^2$, so that the area of the annulus is $3\sqrt{}r^2$. Due to soil relocation, the height of the platform from the ground is therefore three times the depth of the annulus. The depth of the moat is then a fourth part of the pole span, namely $\sqrt{3}r/2$ feet$=6\sqrt{3}$ feet.

49. Library Logic

The order was *After-Dinner Insults, Evenings in the Bath, Faking a Heart Attack, Desert Pub Crawl, Cruel Cake Recipes, Baking a Brick,* and *Grandma the Pole-vaulter.*

Taking the first letter of each book, write down the four ways that D—G can fit into the seven places. Then fit E-B, E—B, E——B into each of these so that two spaces, two places apart, are left for A and F. There are sixteen possibilities, but only the solution has exactly three books correctly positioned.

50. Untying the Knot

10 A.M.	Bernie Witless	Irma Fiddle	Royal room
11 A.M.	Danny Hogwash	Lorna Boggle	Smoochy room
12 noon	Colin Popple	Jenny Peebles	Happy room
1 P.M.	Arnold Rumble	Karen Grumble	Cupid room

Danny can only be married at 11 A.M. or 12 noon, because of his temporal relation to Irma and the possibilities for 1 P.M. For the first case, Mr. Rumble can be at 11 A.M. or 1 P.M.; for the second case, he can be at 10 A.M. or 1 P.M. Both the first case at 11 A.M. and the second case at 10 A.M. give the Smoochy room to be used at 1 P.M., which does not permit Miss Grumble to fit in.

For the second case at 1 P.M., we deduce the chronological order for the rooms to be Smoochy, Royal, Happy, Cupid with more than one correct on the list. With the first case at 1 P.M., the order is Royal, Smoochy, Happy, Cupid, which correctly allows only one correct item on the list for the room.

When it comes to the groom's first name, Danny is at 11 A.M. and Colin must be at 12 noon, so is correctly positioned (and the others are not). Bernie can only be at 10 A.M. with Arnold at 1 P.M. We now know that Miss Grumble, who is not with Colin and is sometime after the Smoochy room, can only be at 1 P.M.

The deductions for each column now rely on identifying the correct item in the given list from the already deduced items, and realizing that all other items in that column are wrongly positioned. This gives the correct order.

51. Parking Space

1	Dib	Babbles	Outagas	Blip
2	Jim	Dinoblobs	Runsoncole	Luminus
3	Wop	Monopips	Boldleego	Delta
4	Fud	Fiddlypoos	Geegeepuld	Vulcan

The relation (1) beginning "The spaceship from Delta . . ." can only be first or third, since in second place no spaceship fits and in fourth place no planet fits. The relation (2) beginning "Wop was from neither Blip nor Vulcan . . ." can only be second or third, since first place allows no species and fourth place permits no planet.

If relation (1) is first then relation (3) ". . . and the Babble that captained Outagas . . ." can only be fourth, since in first place no captain is possible, in second place no spaceship fits, and in third place no species fits. So then Outagas is fourth and Boldleego is first. However, there are then no places given correctly for the spaceship (exactly one must be correct). So relation (1) is not first and can only be third.

Relation (3) can now either be first or fourth, since in second place no spaceship is possible and in third place no species is possible. If relation (3) is fourth, the Babble is fourth and the Dinoblob must be first. This gives no species correctly placed. So relation (3) is first.

We now deduce the column positions. For the captain, if Wop is second, then Fud is third (not allowed), so relation (2) with Wop is third and either Dib or Jim is first. Positions 2 and 3 are given wrongly so either position 1 or 4 is correct. If position 4 is right, then Jim is fourth, Dib is not first, and there can be no first position. So position 1 is correct and Dib is first, Wop third, Jim second, Fud fourth.

For the species, we know that a Babble is first and either a Monopip or a Fiddlypoo is third. So the first three given places are wrong, and the Fiddlypoo must be correct in fourth place. Hence the Monopip is third and the Dinoblob is second.

For the spaceship, we know that Outagas is first, so Boldleego must be correctly positioned at third. So Runsoncole is second and Geegeepuld is fourth.

Finally, for the planet, we know that Delta is third and either Blip or Vulcan is fourth. This gives the last three places as wrong, so Blip is first, Vulcan fourth, and Luminus second.
Many congratulations if you got it right!

52. *Introduction*

And finally, the two puzzles in the introduction both work on the principle of substituting each letter in SQUARE and TETRAHEDRON with its position in the alphabet, then totaling the numbers. SQUARE sums to 81, so square is a square, and TETRA and HEDRON both sum to 64, two identical cubes!